The
ELEPHANT
in the ROOM

CHRISSY HIGHTOWER-WILLIS

Cover Art–Kashif Qasim
Book Design–Sharon Kizziah-Holmes

CWP INDIE PRESS

Springdale, Arkansas

ISBN: 978-1-966675-01-3 (Paperback)
ISBN: 978-1-966675-02-0 (eBook)

DEDICATION

To all the aspiring indie authors in the world.
Never give up your dream!

TABLE OF CONTENTS

INTRODUCTION

Let me share my story before we begin this journey together. I am the author of 19 traditionally published nonfiction books, five beloved children's stories, and five independently published works.

My path has woven through the halls of a prominent publisher of teacher resources and a small traditional publishing house. I want to share with you my triumphs and failures.

Let me be clear that I do not identify as a self-published author. There is a distinction between self-publishing and independent publishing. I see myself as an independently published author.

Self-publishing, as its name implies, is a straightforward endeavor. You take the reins to publish your book, overseeing everything from editing to design, marketing to uploading. You may seek the counsel of a distant relative with a flair for English or hire a designer from the vast realms of the internet for a modest fee. Yet, ultimately, your book remains a solitary venture—if fortune smiles, you may sell a handful of copies to friends and family. In my eyes, this positions you as a hobbyist or 'passion writer.' You are a self-published writer, meaning you did it yourself with minimal help from others. While that path has merits, this book does not delve into that realm.

On the other hand, an independently published author embraces the full spectrum of tasks traditionally handled by a publisher but does so with an a-la-carte approach. What separates the two? The self-published author often releases a product that lacks market readiness and has many avoidable errors, a haphazard layout, and a copyright page with a homemade look and feel. I have even seen self-published writers brag about the 'free' ISBN they got from Amazon. That alone tells me the writer has no idea about distribution and no clue that getting the 'free' ISBN has limited their audience and ensured no bookstore, library or school will buy their book.

This book aspires to be your guiding star through the intricate cosmos of publishing as an indie author—a professional who crafts captivating fiction and nonfiction. I want you to become a proud professional in a competitive and ever-evolving marketplace.

So why is the title *The Elephant in the Room*? When we talk about the elephant in the room, it is a phrase used to describe the one thing no one is talking about. That elephant should be evident, but it is overlooked. The elephant in the room for this book's purpose is that writing a book is the beginning, not the end, of your journey as an author. Once the book is written, you are just starting on the road to publication.

If you are poised to begin a journey toward indie authorship, this book is written just for you!

CHAPTER 1

Traditional Publishing vs. Independent Publishing

The Evolution of Indie Publishing

The evolution of indie publishing involves a remarkable journey from self-publishing with a vanity press to a mainstream option for authors. Historically, indie publishing was often associated with vanity presses. As its name implies, a vanity press charges hefty fees for minimal services, leading to a less-than-professional product. Most vanity presses make more money from what they charge authors to publish their books than they do from book sales. In addition, if the author wants to buy books for a show or book signing, once again, they pay a hefty fee to buy author copies from the vanity press.

Through time, vanity presses have become even more sophisticated in their marketing efforts, naming their company something that might trick an author into believing they are publishing with a legitimate publisher—for example, Harper-Collin Publishing or Amazon Press.

Suppose you receive an email asking you to publish your book sight unseen, or a promise to make you the next New York Times Best-Selling Author by publishing with their company. Your best course of action is to DELETE the email. Legitimate publishers do not reach out to unknown writers via email. I've heard horror stories about writers paying thousands of dollars to get their book published, only to discover there is no marketing, distribution, or support once the book is out.

The hybrid publisher is a new player in the publishing industry. In recent years, hybrid publishing has experienced significant growth. It's self-publishing that appears more professional. In this model, both the author and the publisher share the costs of publication and, theoretically, the profits. This cost-sharing setup is often called 'author subsidized publishing' when referring to a hybrid publisher. Hybrid publishers usually provide a more comprehensive distribution process and higher quality editing and book design compared to vanity presses. However, it's important to recognize that, like any industry, there are both reputable and questionable hybrid publishers.

Digital Platforms Reshaped the Publishing Industry

With the rise of digital platforms, indie publishing gained traction in the early 2000s. E-readers and online marketplaces, such as Amazon Kindle Direct Publishing, revolutionized how books were distributed and consumed. Authors no longer needed to print thousands of physical copies; instead, they could publish their work with just a few clicks. The concept of POD (Print on Demand) drastically changed the industry. This accessibility empowered authors to share their stories and enabled them to retain a larger share of the profits. As a result, many writers began to explore this avenue, leading to a surge in independently published titles.

The quality of indie-published works has significantly improved over the years, thanks to the availability of professional editing, design, and marketing services. Authors are now more informed and equipped with tools to enhance and present their manuscripts professionally. The emergence of online courses, webinars, and writing communities has further supported authors in honing their craft and understanding the intricacies of the publishing process. Consequently, self-publishing has morphed into independently published books. Indie-published books have gained legitimacy, attracting attention from readers, critics, and even traditional publishers. As an indie author, you have a wealth of resources to help you succeed.

Besides quality improvements, the rise of social media has transformed how authors build their brands and connect with readers. Platforms like Instagram, X, and Facebook provide authors with a direct line to their audience, allowing them to share their writing journey, engage with fans, and promote their works. This shift has made it easier for authors to carve out niche markets, targeting specific demographics and interests. Building a personal brand has become essential for indie-published authors, as it fosters loyalty and encourages word-of-mouth marketing.

Today, indie publishing is no longer just a viable alternative to traditional publishing; it has become a thriving industry.

Authors who choose this route are often more empowered, taking control of their creative visions and business decisions. The landscape continues to develop, with technological advancements like AI-powered editing tools, virtual book tours, and marketing strategies such as influencer partnerships. Targeted social media ads are shaping the future of book sales. As authors navigate this dynamic environment, they can draw lessons from the past to succeed in their publishing efforts.

Authors can now bypass traditional gatekeepers like literary agents and publishing houses and take control of their work. This change has revolutionized the publishing process and allowed a broader range of voices and stories to reach audiences. Where once an author's only options were a traditional publisher, a small publishing company, or paying a lot of money to a vanity press, it's now, in some ways, the Wild West out there. The options are endless, and as an indie author, you have the freedom to express your creativity and tell your story in your own way. This empowerment gives you the confidence to navigate the publishing world on your own terms.

Key Differences Between Traditional and Indie Publishing

Traditional publishing and self-publishing, now often called indie publishing, are two different routes for authors to bring their works to the market, each with its own benefits and challenges. Traditional publishing usually involves a publisher handling the editing, designing, producing, and distribution of a book. This process often requires an author to find an agent and go through a competitive and lengthy selection process. On the other hand, indie publishing allows authors to keep complete control over their work, enabling them to make decisions about everything from cover design to pricing and marketing. However, with this freedom comes responsibility, and indie authors need to be informed and willing to pay for the services needed to produce a high-quality book.

One of the most significant differences lies in the financial aspects of each model.

In traditional publishing, authors usually receive an advance against future royalties, which can provide some immediate financial support. However, it is essential to note that an advance is a payment toward future sales, and you will not receive another penny until you have sold enough books to repay that advance. Small traditional publishers rarely give advances. In both cases, authors receive a royalty, or a percentage of the books sold. This percentage varies from 8% to 10%.

Traditional publishers often make substantial profits, leaving authors with a smaller revenue share. Indie publishing, on the other hand, can offer higher profit margins since authors retain a more significant portion of the sales proceeds. This financial independence can be appealing, especially for those willing to invest time and resources in marketing their books. As an indie author, you have the potential to earn more from your hard work, giving you a sense of financial security and control over your earnings.

Small presses, considered traditional publishers, typically offer many services that much larger presses offer. However, while most small presses are legitimate, some are not. Some small publishing houses present themselves as traditional, but their contracts are full of loopholes, such as hefty fees to get your rights back even if they fail to publish your book on time, or offer a large royalty percentage, such as 60% of net. Beware if a contract has these things in it, because their definition of net may mean you get 60% of what is left over after they recover all their costs.

Unless your traditionally published book is a runaway bestseller, a traditional publisher typically will only promote and market said book while it is on their 'front' list. This means that in the first year or maybe two years after the book comes out, you may find yourself with a publicist and marketing team, and depending on the advertising budget, a few ads may be created for your book. Once the book is no longer a 'frontlist', all those responsibilities fall on you as your 'traditional' publisher moves on to the next new book.

Independently published authors take on the financial responsibility up front, and then all the royalties and proceeds go to the author. This allows you to control the costs of your project and reap all the rewards.

It is important to note that neither Kindle Direct Publishing (KDP) nor IngramSpark charges a fee to publish your book. Any company that tells you differently is not only wrong but probably is not reputable and does not have your best interest at heart.

The timeline for publishing also differs significantly between the two methods.

Traditional publishing can involve a lengthy process, often taking months or even years from acceptance to release. This timeline includes multiple rounds of editing, design, and marketing preparation. You rarely have any input on the cover design; sometimes, a traditional publisher might delete parts of your book that you feel are important.

Just how long does it take? Well, it depends on the publisher. Many traditional publishers only accept agented submissions, and acquiring an agent takes time and effort. That is why I cannot emphasize enough the importance of making connections and going to writing conferences and seminars, especially if they have agents. Typically, at a live event, an agent might take pitches from participants, and if you are lucky, that agent may ask you to send them more information. If that happens, follow up immediately. Keep in mind that an agent should never charge you to review your work. Legitimate agents are always looking for clients, but the market is so competitive that it is hard to acquire an agent.

But let's pretend your book is accepted by a publisher (large, medium, or small). From the time you sign the contract (which you had an intellectual property lawyer review carefully) to when the book comes out, it will be 2 to 3 years on average.

Independent publishing allows for a much quicker turnaround, enabling authors to publish their work as soon as it is ready. This speed can be advantageous in niche markets where trends change rapidly, and timely releases can more effectively capture audience interest. It also allows you to set your release date. For example, my children's book about the first pioneer woman to climb Pikes Peak was released close to the anniversary of that time, giving me additional opportunities to market and sell the book.

Marketing and distribution strategies are another area where traditional and indie publishing diverge.

Traditional publishers typically have established relationships with retailers and distribution networks, which can facilitate wider exposure for a book. However, authors may have limited say in marketing their books. In contrast, indie-published authors handle their marketing efforts, which can be both a challenge and an opportunity. This autonomy allows authors to tailor their marketing strategies to their specific audience and develop a unique author brand that resonates with readers.

Smaller presses often have limited funds to help with marketing, so other than putting your book on their website, you, the author, are still responsible for marketing a book where your profit margin may be small.

Finally, the creative control experienced by indie-published authors can be a double-edged sword.

While the ability to make creative decisions fosters a sense of ownership and personal expression, it also requires authors to be well-informed about the publishing process and market trends. Traditional publishers offer guidance and resources, which can benefit less experienced authors. Ultimately, choosing between traditional and indie publishing depends on an author's individual goals, resources, and willingness to navigate the challenges of the publishing landscape. Each path has its advantages, and understanding the key differences can help authors make informed decisions about their publishing journey.

The Benefits of Going Solo

Indie publishing is a gateway to a world of empowerment and inspiration for authors. It offers a plethora of benefits that can significantly enhance their writing careers.

One of the most interesting advantages of indie publishing is the level of creative control it affords. Authors who publish indie can maintain their unique voice and vision throughout the process, from manuscript development to cover design and marketing strategies. This autonomy allows writers to bring their stories to life exactly as they envision without conforming to traditional publishers' demands or preferences. This control can be particularly beneficial for niche authors, as they can tailor their content and branding to resonate specifically with their target audience.

Another significant benefit of indie publishing is the potential for higher financial returns.

Traditional publishing models often involve sharing profits with agents and publishers, which can significantly diminish an author's earnings. In contrast, independently published authors typically retain a more substantial percentage of their royalties, especially when selling through platforms that offer favorable terms. This financial independence can empower authors to reinvest their earnings into further projects or marketing efforts, ultimately allowing them to grow their brand and reach a broader audience.

Indie publishing enables authors to respond quickly to market trends and reader feedback.

Unlike traditional publishing, where the timeline can span several months or even years, indie publishing allows immediate adjustments. Suppose an author identifies a growing trend in their niche market or receives constructive feedback from readers. In that case, they can quickly revise their work or launch new titles that capitalize on these insights. This agility is a significant advantage in today's fast-paced marketplace, where reader preferences can shift rapidly.

Building an author's brand becomes significantly more straightforward when going solo.

Authors can craft their public persona and marketing strategy without the constraints often imposed by traditional publishers. They can engage directly with their audience through social media, newsletters, and personal websites, fostering a deeper connection with readers. This direct interaction helps promote their current titles but also helps understand their audience's preferences, which can inform future writing projects and branding efforts.

Lastly, going solo promotes a sense of community and collaboration among authors.

Many indie-published writers find it beneficial to connect

with others in similar niches and share experiences, tips, and resources. This collaborative spirit can lead to opportunities for joint ventures, cross-promotions, and support networks that enhance visibility and credibility. By embracing the indie publishing journey, authors take charge of their careers and contribute to a growing community of independent writers redefining the publishing landscape.

It is also important to remember that indie authors are a very supportive community. When you join a genre group or critique group, you build connections that not only improve your writing but also expand your network. Learning from others helps you refine your skills and stay engaged with like-minded people.

How do you build this community? Look for organizations related to your genre. If you are a children's book author, consider joining the Society of Children's Book Writers and Illustrators (SCBWI). There are state chapters, and often SCBWI offers webinars free to members. If you want to write western novels, then consider joining Western Writers of America (WWA). No matter what you are interested in writing, you will find there is likely a group or organization dedicated to that genre.

The Elephant's Trunk

(Important points from the chapter)

1. The publishing landscape has evolved, and independent publishing is now viable.
2. Traditional, hybrid, and independent publishing have pros and cons.

3. Authors must carefully research all their options before deciding which route works best for them.

CHAPTER 2

The Business of Writing

Treating Your Writing as a Business

Treating your writing as a business is crucial in today's rapidly changing literary world. Many authors see writing as just a passion project, but adopting a professional mindset is key to succeeding in indie publishing. This means recognizing that writing isn't only about creativity; it also involves strategy, marketing, and financial management. By viewing your writing as a business, you can better handle the challenges of indie publishing and set yourself up for long-term success.

1. Establishing clear goals is the first step in treating your writing as a business. Defining what success looks like for you, whether it's a specific income level, a specific number of books sold, or growing your readership, provides a clear direction for your writing career. These goals will guide your decision-making and help you assess your

progress, keeping you focused and determined on your path to success.

2. Understanding your target audience and niche market is crucial to treating your writing as a business. Researching your genre and identifying your readers' preferences and needs will inform your writing, marketing strategies, and branding efforts. By focusing on a specific audience, you can tailor your content and promotional tactics to resonate with them, increasing your chances of achieving commercial success in the competitive literary landscape.

3. Building an author brand (Chapter 6) is another critical component of treating your writing as a business. Your brand encompasses your unique voice, style, and the themes that permeate your work. It also includes your online presence, website, and social media profiles. Invest time creating a cohesive and professional brand that reflects your identity as an author. Engage with your audience through various platforms, showcasing your writing, personality, and expertise. This connection fosters loyalty and increases the likelihood that readers will purchase and recommend your books to others.

4. Managing the financial aspects of your writing business is vital to treating your writing as a business. Keeping track of your expenses and income, and understanding the costs associated with indie publishing, including editing, cover design, marketing, and distribution, is essential. By

developing a budget that accounts for these expenses and setting aside funds for future projects, you can ensure the sustainability of your writing career. Keeping records of your costs can be beneficial at tax time, as many of your writer-related expenses can be tax deductible.

5. Explore ways to diversify your income streams, such as offering workshops, speaking engagements, or merchandise related to your books. By treating your writing as a business and implementing sound financial practices, you can create a sustainable career that allows you to thrive in indie publishing.

Understanding Publishing Options (I'm repeating it!)

Understanding the publishing landscape is crucial for authors to navigate the path from manuscript to marketplace. With various options available, it is essential to comprehend the differences between traditional, hybrid, and indie publishing. Each route offers distinct advantages and challenges, influencing how authors approach their work, manage their time, and allocate their financial resources. By understanding these options, authors can make informed decisions that align with their goals and target audience, empowering them to take control of their publishing journey.

1. Traditional publishing involves submitting a manuscript to a publishing house. Here, an editor evaluates it for potential publication. This route can provide authors with professional editing,

marketing, and distribution support, often resulting in broader reach and credibility. However, traditional publishing can be lengthy and competitive, requiring authors to surrender a significant portion of their creative control and profits. Understanding these trade-offs is vital for authors who prioritize recognition and support over complete autonomy.

2. Hybrid publishing has emerged as a middle ground, blending traditional and indie publishing elements. In this model, authors pay for certain services, such as editing and design, while retaining a degree of control over their work. This approach can offer a faster route to publication and a more significant share of royalties than traditional publishing. However, authors must carefully research hybrid publishers to ensure their practices are reputable and transparent. In addition, authors must learn to recognize when a hybrid publisher is legitimate and when it is not. This understanding helps authors align their expectations and avoid potential pitfalls. Another challenge of hybrid publishing is that the contract often requires authors to order large numbers of their books at the publisher's cost. Some authors have found that selling books at an inflated price to authors is how some hybrid publishers make the bulk of their profits.

3. It has been previously mentioned, and it will be reiterated here, that self-publishing and indie publishing are **NOT** the same. Self-publishing involves a total do-it-yourself approach. Whereas

indie publishing is done using professional help, i.e. editors, cover and book designers, etc. It has gained immense traction in recent years, while still allowing authors complete control over their work and the publishing process. With platforms like Kindle Direct Publishing, IngramSpark, and others, authors can easily publish and distribute their books, eliminating the need for a traditional publisher. This route empowers authors to set their pricing, market their work, and build their brand according to their vision. However, indie publishing also requires authors to take on the responsibilities of marketing, distribution, and quality control, necessitating a solid understanding of the business aspects of writing.

Ultimately, the choice of publishing option depends on an author's goals, resources, and desired level of involvement in the publishing process. By thoroughly understanding the nuances of each option, authors can craft a strategy that aligns with their objectives and enhances their chances of success in the competitive marketplace. Whether aiming for the prestige of traditional publishing, the flexibility of hybrid publishing, or the autonomy of indie publishing, informed decision-making is vital for authors seeking to establish a lasting presence in their chosen niche.

Financial Considerations

Financial considerations play a crucial role in the indie publishing journey, influencing both the quality of the final product and the potential for profitability. Authors must first assess their budget, understanding that indie publishing involves various costs, including editing, cover design, formatting, and marketing. Setting a realistic budget allows authors to allocate funds appropriately and avoid overspending in areas that may not yield a significant return on investment. Authors need to research the average costs associated with each aspect of indie publishing to develop a comprehensive financial plan. Please see the resource section for suggestions on creating a book budget.

Investing in professional editing is one of the most critical financial decisions an author can make (see Chapter 4). Quality editing enhances a manuscript's readability and overall appeal, which can significantly affect sales. While some authors may attempt to self-edit to save costs, this often results in a subpar product. Authors should consider hiring freelance editors or utilizing editing services that fit within their budget. Allocating a portion of the budget to editing can lead to higher reader satisfaction and better reviews, ultimately contributing to the book's success in the marketplace.

1. There is more than one type of editing, and it is prudent that the indie author knows the difference between developmental, content, and line editing. A developmental editor looks at the overall arc of your story and how you develop the plot, and a

content editor looks for all content-related aspects. After both processes are complete, a line editor or proofreader should be the final eyes on the book. While the content and developmental editor may be the same person, the line editor needs to be a professional whose only job is to look for grammar, syntax, and style mistakes. **A retired English teacher, your cousin majoring in creative writing, or your critique group, while somewhat helpful, does not meet the requirements to proofread your book.**

2. Cover design is another vital financial consideration affecting an author's sales potential. A professionally designed cover can entice readers and create a strong first impression, while a poorly designed cover may deter potential buyers. Authors should research designers specializing in their book's genre and request previous work samples. Investing in a high-quality cover design can be decisive in attracting readers and establishing an author brand. Authors must weigh design costs against the potential benefits of increased visibility and sales.

3. Marketing is essential to indie publishing, often requiring a significant financial investment. Authors must develop marketing strategies that include social media advertising, email marketing, and collaborations with influencers or bloggers in their niche. Each marketing avenue comes with its own set of costs, and authors should evaluate which methods are likely to yield

the best results based on their target audience. A well-executed marketing plan can enhance book visibility, drive sales, and ultimately provide a return on investment that justifies the initial expenditure. Marketing starts well before the book is published, and a well-planned marketing campaign can make the difference between success and failure.

Authors should consider ongoing financial management as part of their ongoing publishing journey. Taxes are a consideration for the author, and if you do not use a CPA, preferably one who understands intellectual property, I encourage you to do so. In your writing, there is a lot of information about whether you should incorporate or form a limited liability company (LLC). I am not a tax professional, nor would I attempt to give you tax advice, but I would encourage you to research. There are pros and cons to each.

This includes tracking expenses, setting pricing strategies, and analyzing sales data to make informed decisions about future projects. Tools such as spreadsheets or accounting software can help authors clarify their financial situation. Understanding the economic aspects of indie publishing not only empowers authors to make informed choices but also equips them with the knowledge to build a sustainable career in writing. By being mindful of their financial decisions, authors can maximize their chances of success in the competitive indie publishing landscape, fostering a sense of optimism and motivation.

The Elephant's Trunk

1. Writing is a business; treat it like one!
2. Understand the financial considerations of running a business.
3. Create a well-thought-out business plan.

CHAPTER 3

Writing for Niche Markets

Identifying Your Niche

Identifying your niche is a crucial step in your indie publishing journey. A niche is a specific market segment that caters to a particular audience's interests and needs. A genre is a broader category that classifies your book based on its content, style, and form. Understanding this distinction is vital for authors as it allows targeted marketing efforts, increases visibility, and enhances the potential for sales.

Finding your niche (often called your genre) involves more than deciding whether to write fiction or nonfiction. Broad genres include romance, science fiction, children's books, speculative fiction, mystery, true crime, and westerns. Each genre has sub-genres such as historical, contemporary, cozy mystery, sweet romance, etc. In nonfiction, it may be a how-to book, a memoir, a biography, or an educational book. Some authors, like me, are lucky to write in both areas, but reading and learning about specific genres is essential, regardless of what you want to write.

Here is a list of some of the major genres. It is not meant to be all-inclusive but to give you an idea of what types of books you might want to write.

Fiction

Action & Adventure—Your central character encounters many potentially dangerous and life-threatening challenges on the path to achieving their goal.

Children's Books—Children's books may range from picture books for young children to easy readers for elementary-age children. They also include middle-grade fiction, which may have more detail in the plot and more elements of mystery.

Contemporary—Takes place in current times and involves day-to-day things like financial struggles or handling job loss.

Crime Thriller—This genre combines crime with suspense. While we may not see the actual crime committed, the characters face obstacles and challenges as they deal with a whodunnit or a psychopathic killer on the loose. While a crime thriller does not have to include graphic violence, it is acceptable in this genre.

Mystery—There are two components: a crime or mystery to solve, and a professional or amateur hunting for the solution. The story can fall under various sub-genres, from hard-boiled or romantic suspense to cozy or police procedurals.

Dystopian—A popular sub-genre of science fiction, the story is set in the future (near or years from now) where life is dark and sad, and a happy outcome is not assured, and often has undertones of cultural or social issues that to some extent we are grappling with today.

Fantasy—Elements of magic or the supernatural are woven into the story, and it may involve world-building. It is often inspired by mythology or folklore.

Historical—While the story is fiction, it is set in a specific period with historically accurate details and may include real people or actual events. With the internet, it is now critically important that if you are writing a historical novel; you are meticulous about place, time, and events.

Horror/Thriller—The story can be set in any period and a real or imagined setting, and doesn't require a specific type of plot. It does need to scare readers, yet keep them turning the page until the denouement. Horror stories usually involve physical fear, while thrillers are more psychological. Still, both are about the character trying to save their own life or the life of someone they love.

LGBTQ+—Stories in this category aren't limited to a specific genre (think romance or sci-fi) but do require that the LGBTQ+ characters are featured in the main plot.

Literary Fiction—This category requires character-driven stories that are not plot-driven and have a more serious and introspective tone.

Mystery—A very popular genre that requires two components: a crime or mystery to solve, and a professional or amateur hunting for the solution. The story can fall under various sub-genres, from hard-boiled or romantic suspense to cozy or police procedurals.

New Adult—These stories feature characters who are out of adolescence and anywhere from 18 to early 30s, and they explore themes such as establishing one's identity, making career choices, gaining independence, and exploring sexuality.

Paranormal—A paranormal novel has elements of the supernatural and characters with magical or supernatural traits. It might also contain supernatural or phantasmagorical events and a timeline that doesn't follow a direct chronological order but can shift from past to present.

Romance—While it can have elements of other genres (think mystery, suspense or historical), the storyline is front-and-center a romance: Character A and Character B fall in love, something intervenes, they find their way back together, and live happily ever after (aka, HEA) or at least Happily For Now (HFN). Romances can be sweet with very little sex involved or spicy with more explicit sexual matter.

Science Fiction—Unlike fantasy, these stories feature an imagined future based on genuine science or technological advances, or the possibility that these could develop given current advances.

Speculative Fiction—Is an umbrella term for genres that explore possibilities beyond everyday reality, encompassing science fiction, fantasy, horror, and more, often asking "what if" questions. Such as, "what if you wake up in the morning and suddenly find that you are the only person left on planet earth?"

Supernatural—This category is typified by elements beyond scientific understanding, events that don't adhere to real-world rules. It features characters from folklore and fairy tales (e.g., fairies, aliens, shapeshifters, angels, ghosts, etc.).

Suspense—Not quite to the thriller level — these stories generate frightened anticipation in the reader. Storylines can include elements from other genres (like romance or crime, for example).

Women's Fiction—The main component of women's fiction is a strong female protagonist, with or without a love interest (which is secondary), and other female characters. The focus is on the main character's emotional and/or psychological development, who can be any age. The readership of this genre is primarily women.

Young Adult—The storyline and reading level are geared to those 12 to 18 (although adults may also enjoy the stories), with a worldview and adolescent challenges typical of that age bracket.

Nonfiction—is writing that includes all books that aren't based on a fictional narrative.

Below is a list of some significant types of nonfiction:

- Academic text
- Autobiography
- Biography
- History

- How-To
- Humor
- Memoir
- Philosophy
- Self-help
- Travel guide

Regardless of what you decide to write, it is essential that you get acquainted with and research that genre.

What to Do Next?

Read books in the genre you are interested in writing. Don't just read all the bestsellers; read various books to determine the rules. Yes, there are rules, such as the difference between a mystery and a cozy mystery. The difference between a 'spicy' romance and a 'sweet' (think Hallmark channel) romance. Also, remember that what is 'hot' this year might not be so hot next year.

Join organizations that cater to your genre. It is worth repeating here again: if you want to write westerns, look into Western Writers of America. For children's books, join the Society of Children's Book Writers and Illustrators (SCBWI) or the Society for Children's Picture Books. You get the general idea.

Next, find a tribe, whether it's a critique group, a writer's group, or a good writers' conference. This is where you learn more about your craft. Writers are some of the most supportive people in the world, so develop relationships. Remember, you are not out copying someone else's style; you want to build your own unique voice.

To effectively identify your niche, consider your interests, expertise, and the unique perspective you bring to the table. Reflecting on your experiences and passions will help you create an authentic and sustainable space.

Begin by conducting thorough market research. Explore existing books within your potential niches to gauge their popularity and identify gaps in the market. Tools like online bookstores, genre bestsellers, and social media platforms can provide insights into current trends and reader preferences. Please pay attention to reader reviews and feedback, as this information can illuminate what audiences seek and feel is missing. This analysis will help you pinpoint a profitable niche and inform your writing style and content.

Once you understand the market landscape, create a reader persona that embodies your ideal audience. Consider demographics such as age, gender, interests, and reading habits. This persona will guide your writing and marketing processes, ensuring your content resonates with your target readers. By focusing on a specific audience, you can tailor your messaging, cover design, and promotional strategies to appeal to their preferences and needs.

Building an author brand (see Chapter 6) is intimately tied to your niche. Your brand should reflect your identity as a writer and the unique value you offer within your chosen niche. This involves crafting an interesting author bio, developing a cohesive visual identity for your book covers and promotional materials, and establishing a consistent voice across your platforms. A strong author brand attracts readers and fosters community around your work, encouraging loyal followership and engagement.

Finally, be open to revisiting and refining your niche as you grow as an author. The publishing landscape is dynamic, and reader preferences can shift over time. Stay attuned to industry trends, engage with your audience through social media and author events, and remain flexible. By continuously evaluating and adapting your niche, you can ensure that your work remains relevant and appealing, ultimately paving the way for long-term success in the indie publishing marketplace.

Tailoring Content to Audience Needs

Understanding your audience is crucial for authors looking to significantly affect the indie publishing market. Tailoring content to meet the unique needs of your readers not only enhances engagement but also fosters loyalty and encourages word-of-mouth promotion. By identifying your target audience's preferences and interests, you can create content that resonates deeply, leading to higher sales and a stronger author brand. This process begins with thorough research into the demographics and psychographics of your potential readers.

Once you clearly understand your audience, the next step is to align your writing style and tone with their expectations. For example, if you target a business audience, using formal language, providing data-driven insights, and incorporating case studies will probably be more effective than a casual, narrative style. Conversely, a lighthearted tone may work well for the self-help or personal development genres. Adapting your voice makes your work more relatable and demonstrates that you value your readers' preferences.

Besides style, the content must address your audience's specific needs and challenges. This means focusing on topics that matter to them and providing actionable solutions. For instance, if you are writing for aspiring entrepreneurs, consider discussing practical strategies for business growth, marketing, or financial management. Including real-world examples and case studies can enhance credibility and show readers that you understand their struggles and aspirations. This targeted approach ensures that your writing remains relevant and valuable.

Another important aspect of tailoring content is the format in which it is presented. Different audiences may prefer formats like eBooks, audiobooks, or blog posts. Understanding these preferences allows you to adapt your material accordingly. For example, busy professionals might appreciate concise, digestible information presented in a checklist or summary format, while readers in creative niches may enjoy more in-depth, narrative-driven content. By diversifying your content delivery, you can reach a wider audience while catering to their unique needs.

Finally, ongoing engagement with your audience is essential for continued success in indie publishing. Utilizing social media platforms, newsletters, and author websites can help you gather feedback and monitor changing interests. This engagement allows you to adjust your content strategy and strengthen your author brand by fostering a community around your work. By staying attuned to your audience and being willing to adapt, you can ensure that your content remains relevant and impactful, ultimately driving your indie publishing success.

Researching Successful Niche Authors

Researching successful niche authors is essential for any aspiring writer looking to discover their place in indie publishing. By analyzing the strategies employed by established authors in specific niches, writers can glean valuable insights into what resonates with readers and what marketing techniques yield positive results. This process examines various elements of an author's career, including their writing style, thematic focus, marketing approaches, and audience engagement methods. By studying these aspects, authors can better understand how to position their work effectively within their chosen niche.

One of the first steps in this research process is identifying successful authors within your niche. This could include those who have achieved bestseller status, garnered significant social media followings, or received prestigious awards. Tools such as Amazon rankings, Goodreads ratings, and author interviews can provide a wealth of information. Please pay attention to their book descriptions, cover designs, and pricing strategies as these elements often play a crucial role in attracting readers. Gathering data on their publication frequency and the types of promotional campaigns they engage in can also highlight trends and best practices that benefit your journey.

Next, it is vital to delve into the content itself. Reading the works of successful niche authors allows you to analyze their writing styles, voices, and thematic choices. Consider the topics they explore and how they present their ideas. This analysis can help you identify gaps in the market or unique angles that you can leverage in your writing. Note their audience engagement—look at their social media interactions, blog posts, and newsletters to understand how they communicate with their readers. This can inspire your strategies for building a loyal readership.

Another essential aspect to consider is these authors' branding. Successful niche authors often have a strong, recognizable brand that differentiates them from the competition. Investigating how they present themselves online through websites and social media profiles can provide insights into effective branding strategies. Look for consistency in their messaging, visuals, and overall persona. This branding helps attract an audience and establishes credibility within the niche. Understanding how to create a cohesive author brand can significantly affect your visibility and appeal to potential readers.

Finally, don't overlook the importance of community engagement and networking among authors in your niche. Many successful authors actively take part in writing groups, workshops, and author events, fostering relationships that can lead to collaborative opportunities.

Critique groups are influential as long as you make sure the people in your group understand your genre and the group is structured to provide honest suggestions to help improve your writing and make your books more marketable. A word of caution about critique groups: while they can be an invaluable resource for an author, it is still an opinion you may or may not choose to follow.

Engaging with fellow authors can provide support, feedback, and additional insights into the industry. By studying how these authors interact with each other and their readers, you can develop strategies for building a network that enhances your indie publishing journey. Embracing these research practices will empower you to navigate the complexities of indie publishing and pave the way for your success in niche markets.

The Elephant's Trunk

1. Identify your niche market, and then research and read books in that genre.
2. Learn how to tailor content to your audience's needs.
3. Get involved with a writer's group, seminars, or critique groups that write in your niche.

CHAPTER 4

Crafting an Interesting Manuscript

The Importance of Editing

Editing is a crucial step in the indie publishing process. It can significantly affect the success of your manuscript. Many authors, particularly those new to the indie publishing world, may underestimate the importance of editing, viewing it merely as a final touch rather than an essential component of the writing process. However, effective editing can mean the difference between a manuscript that resonates with readers and one that falls flat. An unedited manuscript will contain grammatical errors, awkward phrasing, and inconsistencies that can distract or confuse readers, ultimately undermining the author's credibility and brand. If a reader finds your book full of mistakes and errors, it will not only lead to your losing that reader who will never buy future books you write, but it may also lead to said reader writing you a poor review (See Chapter 5). A poorly edited manuscript screams amateur and can affect your readership for years.

The editing process goes beyond mere proofreading; it encompasses multiple stages, including developmental editing, copyediting, and proofreading.

1. Developmental editing focuses on the overall structure and content of the manuscript, ensuring that the narrative flows logically and that character development is coherent. This stage allows authors to refine their ideas and strengthen their arguments, which is especially important for those writing in niche markets where clarity and precision are paramount.
2. Copyediting zeros in on language mechanics, such as grammar, punctuation, and style consistency. While a great writing tool, Grammarly is NOT a substitute for a professional copy editor.
3. Finally, proofreading is the last defense against typos and minor errors that can detract from the reading experience. It is the last step before the manuscript goes to design and formatting and is paramount in preparing your manuscript for publication.

Investing time and resources into editing enhances manuscript quality and plays a vital role in building an author's brand (see Chapter 6). Readers often associate a book's professionalism with its editing quality. A polished manuscript can lead to positive reviews, increased word-of-mouth marketing, and more significant sales, all of which contribute to establishing a strong author brand. Conversely, a poorly edited book can damage an author's reputation, making it challenging to attract a loyal readership. In the competitive world of indie publishing, where countless titles vie for attention, maintaining a professional standard is essential for standing out.

Editing fosters a deeper understanding of one's writing style and voice. Engaging with an editor—whether a professional or a trusted peer—can provide valuable feedback that helps authors recognize their strengths and weaknesses. This constructive criticism is vital for growth, allowing authors to enhance their writing skills. By embracing the editing process, authors become more adept at communicating their ideas and connecting with their audience. This is especially important in niche markets where targeted messaging can influence and significantly impact reader engagement.

Ultimately, the importance of editing cannot be overstated in indie publishing. It serves as a bridge between the initial draft and the final product that readers will engage with. Authors who prioritize editing improve the quality of their work and enhance their chances of success in the indie publishing marketplace. By understanding and valuing the editing process, authors can ensure that their manuscripts are well-written and resonate with their intended audience, paving the way for a successful writing career.

So where do you find an editor? Look at websites, word of mouth, and most importantly the credentials of a potential editor. If you only join one organization as an indie author, I strongly recommend joining The Alliance of Independent Authors (ALLi). ALLi provides a comprehensive vetted service directory that lists reputable editors and other publishing services. You can also access materials to help with marketing and editing as a member. In addition, their watchdog division constantly monitors predatory publishing services and keeps members informed.

Remember, just because someone majored in English in college or likes to read does not make them an editor. Have you ever been reading a book and had to stop because of all the grammatical or syntactical errors? Don't kill off your readers because you edited your manuscript yourself.

I will reiterate that some excellent writing tools, such as Grammarly, AutoCrit, ProWritingAid, Evernote, Reedsy Book Editor, and Ulysses, can help you become a better writer. Still, they do not replace the input from a qualified editor.

Your Title

Believe it or not, your title is crucial to the success of your book. I work with children's book authors, helping them produce award-winning books. One of my authors wrote a cute story about a young child trying to figure out his upcoming surprise, only to discover he was getting a new sibling. The original title was *George's Big Surprise*. As the publishing coordinator for this author, I researched titles and found several titles with the same name, and because of the famous Curious George book series, her book would get lost in the sea of 'George' books. After researching, the author and I collaborated and changed the title to *Liam's Big Surprise*. Not only did the book win awards, but it was positioned much higher in the mystical Amazon world of rankings. My book *Bloomers on Pikes Peak* started with the title *The Story of Julia Archibald Holmes, First Woman to Climb Pikes Peak*. Adding a little sparkle made the new title more appealing to the reader. Your title can mean a reader will pick up your book or walk right by.

I know that a title can't be copyrighted. I recently argued with a person on a Facebook group for children's authors (a weak moment on my part) that naming her book *Goodnight Moon,* while legal, was certainly ill-advised. Your goal is to be unique and grab a reader. If you want to recycle something, a book title is not the place to start. You don't want to be a carbon copy of someone else. You want your unique voice.

Designing an Engaging Cover

An engaging cover is a critical element of indie publishing and can significantly influence a book's marketability. The cover serves as a visual representation of the content, encapsulating the essence of the story or information within. Authors must understand that a well-designed cover attracts potential readers and communicates the book's genre and themes. A reader's first impression of a book often comes from its cover, making it essential to invest time and resources in having a cover designed to embody your book's essence. It is your first marketing tool, so use it wisely. A professional cover designer will know how to create a cover that grabs the reader.

For example, I made up a fictitious book title for fun and asked two online service designers to draw me a cover. Each one charged me $10.

EXAMPLES:

a. / b.

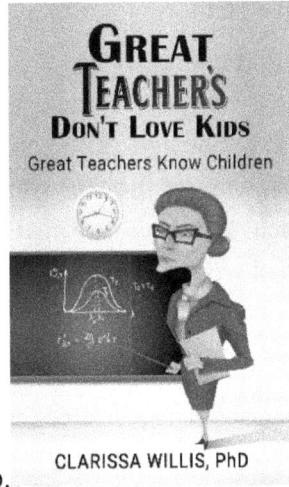

When looking at these two examples, it is easy to note that the designers did not know what the book was about. Example one depicts a man teaching a group of high school students, yet the designer was told the book was about young children. Example two is just a poor cover design that would scare readers away. The teacher looks frightening, and she is teaching math to young children.

When designing a cover, it is crucial to consider the target audience and market niche. In the two examples I showed, you saw neither of these things. The aesthetics that appeal to readers of a romance novel may differ vastly from those attracted to a thriller or a business book. Researching successful titles within a specific genre can provide insight into design trends, color schemes, and typography that resonate with potential buyers. Authors should aim to create a cover that stands out on digital platforms while still fitting comfortably within the expectations of their genre.

Collaboration with a professional designer can elevate a book cover to the next level. While some authors may have graphic design skills, enlisting an expert can ensure that the cover meets industry standards and effectively conveys the book's message. A designer can provide valuable guidance on layout, imagery, and font selection, all of which contribute to the overall impact of the cover. Authors must communicate their vision clearly and be open to feedback during design to achieve the best possible outcome.

Besides visual elements, the title and subtitle play a crucial role in hooking a reader. As mentioned, an interesting title should be memorable, convey the book's essence, and evoke curiosity. The subtitle clarifies the content and attracts the right audience by providing additional context. Authors should also consider how the title will appear on various platforms, including print and digital, to ensure it remains readable and appealing across all mediums.

Finally, authors should test their cover designs before finalizing them. Seeking feedback from beta readers or target audience members can provide insights into how the cover is perceived. A/B testing on different platforms can also help determine which design resonates more effectively with readers. By refining the cover based on real-world feedback, authors can significantly enhance their chances of success in the competitive indie publishing landscape. Do-it-yourself covers look homemade. Unless you have cover design experience, hiring a professional is essential so that your book reflects your vision and represents the story you are writing.

Formatting Your Manuscript for Publication

Formatting your manuscript for publication is a critical step in indie publishing. Proper formatting enhances your work's readability and meets the standards publishers and distributors require. Different platforms have specific guidelines, so understanding the nuances of formatting can significantly affect the presentation of your manuscript. This includes font choice, line spacing, margins, and chapter organization. Authors must familiarize themselves with the requirements of their chosen publishing platforms, such as Amazon Kindle Direct Publishing or IngramSpark, to ensure compliance and aesthetic appeal.

The first element to consider is the font and font size. Most publishers recommend using a standard, easily readable font such as Times New Roman or Arial, typically in a size of 12 points. Consistency is key; your entire manuscript should adhere to the same font style and size. Additionally, setting the correct line spacing—usually 1.5 or double spacing—ensures that your manuscript is easy to read and allows ample space for editors' comments if you choose to work with a professional editor. Margins should be set at one inch on all sides, providing a clean border that enhances readability.

Chapter organization is another vital aspect of manuscript formatting. Each chapter should begin on a new page, often with a clear heading that distinguishes it from the previous section. Utilizing page breaks instead of simply hitting "enter" multiple times improves the structural integrity of the document and maintains consistent spacing. Consider adding a table of contents for longer works, which not only aids navigation but also presents a professional appearance. Moreover, if your manuscript includes images or graphics, ensure they are high resolution and properly aligned within the text to avoid disruptions in the reading flow.

Incorporating front and back matter is essential in manuscript formatting. Front matter typically includes a title page, copyright page, and acknowledgments, while back matter may consist of appendices, a bibliography, or an author bio. This additional content gives readers context and enhances their experience with your book. Furthermore, a well-crafted author bio can establish your brand and connect you with your target audience. It is essential to keep this section concise while highlighting relevant achievements and experiences that lend credibility to your writing.

Lastly, once your manuscript is formatted, it is crucial to conduct a thorough review. This step cannot be overstated; even minor formatting errors can detract from the professionalism of your work. Utilize tools like spell check and grammar check, but also perform a manual read-through to catch any inconsistencies or layout issues. Consider enlisting beta readers or trusted peers to provide feedback on the formatted manuscript. Their insights can reveal how formatting affects the overall reading experience, ensuring your work is polished and ready for publication.

Remember, this is business, and while you may think the product you are selling is your book, in reality, you are the product—your brand, your reputation, and your ability to sell your book to a specific audience. If you plan to write only one book, the writing world is not for you. The rule of thumb is that writers need at least three books published before considering themselves full-time authors.

To Pseudonym or Not to Pseudonym

Because I believe your brand is yourself, I am not a big fan of pseudonyms. Of course, there are exceptions. If, for example, you have established yourself as a paranormal author and you now decide to write a children's book, a pseudonym might be in order. Because I am known as an early childhood author and speaker in the fiction and non-fiction world, I am using a variation of my name for this book.

By doing so, I have decided to establish dual personalities, so to speak: Clarissa Willis, PhD, who writes children's books, curriculum, and nonfiction teacher resource books, and Chrissy Hightower-Willis, who is a bit bohemian and very much non-academic. Will those worlds collide? Only time will tell. Whether or not they do collide, it is going to be fun being a part of both worlds. Only time will tell how that affects my branding.

Hiring an Indie Author Multi-Service Provider

What does an indie author service provider (IASP) do? A service provider is a company that offers various resources a writer needs at an affordable price. Most will assist you with professional editing, cover design, children's book illustrations, and more. They can help you set up your personal print-on-demand (POD) accounts, such as KDP, IngramSpark, D2D, and others. An IASP will also upload your files, handle data entry, and find categories and keywords for your manuscript. They assist with pricing, often supply your ISBN, and allow you to use their professional imprint.

The best way to find a service provider is to go to places like ALLi that maintain a list of reputable companies where you can check credentials. There is also Writers Beware, which keeps up with scams, fake literary agents/agencies, impersonators (someone who might use Amazon in their email address or title when they have no ties to Amazon), and more.

Like anything else, never fully pay for a service before completion. While some companies may require a down payment, with the rest being due upon publication (that is legitimate), an indie author service provider that wants all the money upfront is usually not a company you would like to work with.

Please don't get an indie author multi-service provider mixed up with a vanity press or hybrid publisher. When using an IASP, you keep 100% of your rights and royalties. You purchase your books directly from the POD at a wholesale price, and your royalties are paid directly to you from the POD printer, not the service provider. A service provider will be paid a flat fee that should be quoted before you decide to use the service. There should be no hidden charges.

What services should a reputable Indie Author Multi-Service Provider Offer? *Not every IASP will offer all these.*

- Professional editing services, in-house or freelance
- Top industry-standard formatting for eBook and/or print book (for many platforms)
- Professional cover design, in-house or freelance
- Numerous indie publishing platforms for you to choose from
- Efficient customer service and consistent communication
- One-on-one relationship with your publishing coordinator
- Professional proofreaders
- Willingness to answer all questions about the process
- An open and honest price list
- Personal quotes
- A general service agreement between the company and the author
- Help with needed account(s) setup, i.e. KDP, IngramSpark, Draft2Digital.

WARNING: Watch out for overly expensive formatting services or those demanding payment up front.

10 Questions to Ask Indie Service Providers

1. What rights am I encumbering?
2. Where will my book be distributed and sold?
3. Is your service exclusive or non-exclusive?
4. Who owns the file after publication?
5. Can I make changes to my book after it goes on sale?
6. Do I set my own prices?
7. Is payment an upfront fee, a percentage of sales or both?
8. How do my royalties get paid, and how are they calculated?
9. Are there any extra fees or charges I should know about?
10. Where is the value of my using this service?

(What should an Indie Author Multi-Service Provider offer? and *10 Questions to Ask Indie Author Service Providers* are used with permission from the original author, Sharon Kizziah-Holmes. Thank you, Sharon, for your expertise and guidance.)

Let's move on to online service companies like Fiverr, Behance, and Illustrators for Hire. Here is the bottom line: if you know what you are doing and are specific, you can find good people on these sites. But for every good illustrator on Fiverr, some will use AI and will not give you a quality project. That being said, I have hired two incredible illustrators on Fiverr in the past, and it was a great experience.

One thing I like about Fiverr is that you pay Fiverr upfront (this is an exception to the rule), but the person you hire does not get the money until you are satisfied. If conflicts arise, you can get your money back. One drawback is that once your project is delivered, if you don't request revisions in a timely manner (usually within 48 hours of receiving an email that it has been delivered), they will assume that your project is finished and pay the illustrator.

I own Solander Press (solanderpress.com), and I help authors independently publish books for children and adults in their lives. I don't work with every author who contacts me because I have a vision for Solander Press, and part of that vision is creating children's books that make a difference.

I also recommend Paperback Press (paperback-press.com), another indie author multi-service provider and book design company that helps authors produce market-ready books. Paperback Press has several imprints, including adult fiction, westerns, and thrillers.

When you work with either of these companies, you can use our ISBNs and professional imprints. However, all royalties go directly to you, and you order your author copies directly from KDP, IngramSpark, or the POD company of your choice. All copyrights and materials related to your book belong to you 100%.

The Elephant's Trunk

1. Editing and titling your manuscript are vital to producing a marketable book.

2. Format and book design are key to a professionally presented product.
3. Your book cover is the way to distinguish yourself in a very competitive market.
4. Branding is about selling yourself and not selling a book.

CHAPTER 5

Marketing Your Book

Developing a Marketing Plan

Developing a marketing plan is crucial for authors looking to navigate the world of indie publishing successfully. A well-structured marketing plan helps authors articulate their goals and provides a roadmap for reaching their target audience. To begin, authors should identify their unique selling proposition (USP). This involves understanding what makes their book different from others in the market. By defining USP, authors can communicate their book's value more effectively, making it easier to attract readers seeking specific content within their niche. The best way to determine your USP is what is affectionately called the elevator pitch. If you were on an elevator with a prominent influencer or a person who could promote your book, what would you say in one minute or less to sell them on the idea that your book is the next best seller?

Next, authors should conduct market research. This research will involve analyzing the competition and identifying potential readers. Authors can utilize surveys, social media insights, and online forums to gather information about their target demographic. But they can also ask the reader. If you are writing middle grade fiction, talk to middle grade students. Sherry Roberts, a prominent children and middle-grade author, discovered by accident that middle-graders, especially girls, love to collect pins they can attach to their backpacks. So instead of stickers, which young children adore, she hands out enamel pins to potential readers when she promotes her middle grade series. She understands readers' preferences and interests, as well as the purchasing behaviors of adults in their lives. Good research enables authors to tailor their marketing strategies accordingly. Additionally, identifying similar titles and their successful marketing tactics can provide valuable insights and inspiration for developing an effective plan.

A few free tools help with this research, but do not take the place of experience with the target reader. For example, Kindlepreneur offers a free tool to help with market research. I bought Publishers Rocket for $99, which is not subscription based. This software helps me identify keywords to use, key categories to select, and look at statistics on specific titles that are selling well. As a research tool, it is invaluable in helping an author figure out where to place their book strategically on Amazon. It also lets you know what keywords to use when writing posts and designing marketing materials for your book.

Once the target audience is established, authors should determine the most effective marketing channels to reach that audience. Depending on the niche, this may include social media platforms, email marketing, author websites, and book promotion sites. Each channel has its unique characteristics and audience engagement methods. Authors should choose platforms that resonate with their target market and consider how to leverage them for maximum exposure. Consistency across these channels is key; a cohesive brand message and visual identity will help build recognition and trust among potential readers. However, please post information about more than just your latest book. If all you do is promote your book constantly, people will lose interest quickly. For example, post pictures of yourself traveling solo if your book is about solo travel. If your book is about pets, feature your local animal shelter or post information about pet adoption.

After identifying the channels, authors should set specific, measurable goals for their marketing efforts. Goals could include metrics such as the number of books sold, newsletter sign-ups, social media engagement rates, or website traffic. By establishing these benchmarks, authors can evaluate the effectiveness of their marketing strategies and make necessary adjustments over time. Regularly reviewing progress against these goals will help authors stay focused and motivated, ensuring they remain on track to achieve their objectives.

Finally, authors should remember that marketing is an ongoing effort. Developing a marketing plan is just the beginning; authors must continuously engage with their audience and adapt their strategies to changing market conditions. This could involve periodic reassessments of their marketing tactics, experimenting with new promotional opportunities, or engaging readers through events or book signings. By remaining proactive and flexible, authors can build a strong author brand and foster loyal readership, leading to tremendous success in their indie publishing endeavors.

Utilizing Social Media for Promotion

Social media has transformed how authors promote their work and engage with readers. With platforms like Facebook, X, Instagram, Snapchat, Threads and TikTok, authors can reach a diverse audience, build a community, and create buzz around their books. By effectively leveraging these platforms, authors can increase their visibility and foster relationships vital for long-term success in indie publishing. Understanding the dynamics of each platform is essential for tailoring content that resonates with specific audiences and aligns with personal author branding (see Chapter 6).

Establishing a strong social media presence begins with choosing the right platforms. Authors should consider where their target audience is most active and when they are most active. For instance, visual storytellers might find Instagram an ideal platform for sharing book-related visuals, while nonfiction authors may benefit from LinkedIn for professional networking. Each platform offers unique tools and features, such as Facebook groups for community building or Threads for sharing insights and snippets from their writing process. Authors can maximize engagement and cultivate a loyal following by strategically selecting platforms based on their niche.

1. Content is at the heart of successful social media promotion. Authors should aim to create a diverse mix of posts that include promotional content, personal anecdotes, writing tips, and interactive elements such as polls or Q&A sessions. This blend keeps the audience engaged and encourages them to view the author as a multi-dimensional figure rather than just a bookseller. Additionally, storytelling is a powerful tool; sharing the journey of writing a book, the challenges faced, and the triumphs experienced can create a deeper connection with readers. Being consistent in posting and maintaining a unique voice is crucial for building an author brand that stands out in a crowded marketplace. While something is to be said for shameless self-promotion, too much can be detrimental.

2. Engagement with the audience is another essential component of utilizing social media effectively. Authors should actively respond to comments and messages, fostering community among their followers. Hosting live sessions, participating in book clubs, or collaborating with other authors can enhance visibility and provide opportunities for cross-promotion. Encouraging readers to share their thoughts on the book, participate in challenges, or create user-generated content can also amplify the promotional efforts. By nurturing these interactions, authors can make a dedicated fan base that is more likely to support future projects.

3. Finally, tracking the effectiveness of social media efforts is vital for ongoing improvement. Authors should utilize analytics tools available on various platforms to monitor engagement rates, audience demographics, and content performance. This data can inform future content strategies and help authors refine their promotional approaches. Authors can discover what resonates most with their audience by experimenting with different types of content and posting times. The insights gained from this information can lead to more effective marketing strategies and tremendous success in reaching and expanding the author's readership.

Building an Email List

Building an email list is essential for authors seeking to cultivate a dedicated readership and enhance their indie publishing success. An email list is a direct line of communication between authors and their audience, allowing for personalized engagement and updates. Unlike social media platforms, which can be unpredictable in reach, an email list provides authors with a stable foundation to share news, promotions, and insights directly with their fans. This approach helps build a loyal community and is crucial in marketing new releases and generating pre-sales.

To start building an email list, authors should create a lead magnet, an incentive offered to entice potential subscribers. This could be a free sample chapter of an upcoming book, an exclusive short story, or a downloadable resource related to the author's niche. The key is to ensure that the lead magnet provides genuine value to the reader, making them more likely to sign up. Authors can promote their lead magnets on their websites, social media, and during book signings or events. The goal is to attract subscribers who are genuinely interested in the author's work and are more likely to engage with future content.

Once an email list grows, authors must maintain regular communication with their subscribers. Consistency in messaging helps build trust and keeps readers engaged. Authors should consider sending newsletters with updates on writing progress, insights into the writing process, and tips related to their niche. Additionally, sharing personal anecdotes or behind-the-scenes stories can create a more intimate connection with readers. This sustained engagement encourages loyalty and prompts readers to share the author's content with others, further expanding the email list.

Segmenting the email list can also enhance communication effectiveness. By categorizing subscribers based on their interests or behaviors, authors can tailor their messages to specific groups. For example, a fiction and nonfiction author can segment their list to send targeted information about new releases in each category. This personalized approach increases the likelihood of higher open and click-through rates as subscribers receive content that resonates with their interests. Email marketing tools can aid in this segmentation, making managing and analyzing subscriber behavior easier.

Lastly, authors should regularly evaluate the effectiveness of their email marketing strategies. Analyzing metrics such as open rates, click-through rates, and subscriber growth can provide valuable insights into what resonates with the audience. Based on this feedback, authors should be prepared to adapt their content and approach. Experimenting with different formats, subject lines, and sending frequencies can improve engagement. By continuously refining their email marketing efforts, authors can ensure that their email list remains a powerful tool in building their author brand and achieving indie publishing success.

Other Marketing Strategies

Awards

There are contests, literary awards, and prizes. Contests are events you enter, and you may win a certificate, a badge, or money. Literary awards are more prestigious, and your book must be nominated. Prizes are often given as ribbons or certificates. Until recently, Indie Published authors were banned from some contests, but now many contests support indie authors.

Since it usually costs money to enter a book contest, select one that is reputable and worth your investment. It is a bonus if the entry comes with a critique or book review. The Independent Book Publishers Association (IBPA) formerly offered the Ben Franklin Awards and had numerous categories available to authors. Last year, those awards were renamed the Independent Book Awards. The entry fee is well worth it, and if you are lucky enough to be a finalist, it means free publicity and marketing. In addition, most genre groups have book awards such as the Spur Awards given by the Western Writers of America (no cost to enter and you do not have to be a member to enter), or the RITA Awards presented by the Romance Authors of America.

Other reputable awards include the Next Generation Indie Book Awards and the Independent Book Publisher Association Awards (IPPY). The IPPY Awards are the longest-running unaffiliated contest open exclusively to independent presses.

Endorsements

Endorsements can also greatly enhance your presence in the marketplace. This is particularly true if the endorsement is from a famous writer in your genre or an influencer. For example, when I wrote the nonfiction book *My Child Has Autism* in 2010, a major celebrity had just discovered her child had autism. I got an endorsement from her just by sending her my book.

Endorsements can help with book sales and legitimize you as an author. In addition, it can be a great marketing tool. Think of creative ways to partner with groups in your community. For example, if you write a book about childhood cancer, offer a book signing at your local Ronald McDonald House or Children's Hospital, and donate some proceeds to the organization.

Book Reviews

Book reviews are very important for an author and often challenging to get. Once you get 50 book reviews on Amazon, they help promote your book. However, please beware that you should never review your book or write bogus reviews about it from anonymous people. I have heard horror stories of authors being banned from Amazon for either writing multiple reviews or bad reviews of their competitors' books. I don't pretend to know how Amazon discovers these transgressions, but once you are banned, there is no way to get your account back.

There are some urban legends around book reviews; it is untrue that if your sister buys your book and writes a review, you will be banned. It is also false that you will get banned if your fellow authors purchase and review your book. My favorite myth is that if I typically buy thrillers and buy your children's book to review it, then Amazon will ban the review. It is essential, however, that whoever reviews your book is a verified buyer.

Here are two little tricks I have learned to help garner book reviews. First, I always list my books on Kindle Unlimited. And yes, contrary to what you might read online, you get paid if your books are on Kindle Unlimited. You get paid by the number of pages read. That makes it easier for someone with a Kindle Unlimited account to purchase your book as a verified buyer. In addition, the more products you review, the more likely the book review you write for others will get posted. So, I review the product every time I buy something from Amazon.

Advertisements

It is very easy to spend a lot of money advertising your book only to find that your efforts didn't generate sales. I use Canva to design my book announcements on social media. Before purchasing the full version, try the free version first. Watch a few tutorials; before long, you will make Facebook banners and cover reveal announcements that are eye-catching and professional-looking.

I strongly suggest that you have an author page on social media. I have both an author page and a personal page. To be a professional, it is essential to act like one. Keep politics, off-color jokes, and personal opinions to yourself, even on your personal page. Trust me, people will read both. Even if your page is 'private,' a Facebook tantrum about politics, your ex-boyfriend's antics, or any other controversial subject is unwarranted and will reflect on you as an author.

I often boost Facebook posts. This costs money, so I build a strategic marketing plan to address this. If you pay for an Amazon or Facebook Ad, watch a few tutorials and understand what you are doing.

Do not let them select your demographic when boosting an ad on Facebook. Go in and choose your target audience. Next, ensure the ad you are running is error free and looks professional.

Amazon ads are tricky and based on a bidding system. Understand that you are bidding to see your book by more readers, so learn to be strategic in spending your money.

Building a Strategic Marketing Plan

Three months before the release of my newest children's book, *The Three Little Pigs and the Not So Big Bad Wolf,* I planted the first seed for my readers. I posted a picture from the book of the wolf talking, and with a bit of help from Canva, I created a post that announced the book and gave the tag line, *a new twist on an old story.*

Two months before the book was released, I posted a little more information, and on Thanksgiving, I showed a picture from the book where all the animals were sharing a meal. I then wished my readers and followers a Happy Thanksgiving. I then ordered postcards of the three little pigs and wolf all dressed up for Christmas and sent them to family, friends, and former students.

It was not a sales pitch, just a little information. One month before the book launched, I posted and boosted (paid for an ad) with the cover and a release date. The day the book came out, I posted the cover, a short link to Amazon, and a QR code so readers could click and buy.

I also sent an email blast and asked a good friend with a substantial early childhood following for an endorsement. She endorsed the book and mentioned it in her monthly newsletter. It was the most successful launch, and I had more sales in the first month the book was out than ever before.

In conclusion, marketing is difficult and takes time and effort, but it is well worth it if you are strategic and thoughtful in your planning. Your author brand and marketing plan are interwoven, and in Chapter Six, we will discuss innovative ways to build your author brand.

The Elephant's Trunk

1. Develop a well-thought-out strategic marketing plan.
2. Learn to use social media wisely and intentionally.
3. Build an email list.
4. Look for awards and endorsements that fit your book.
5. Devise innovative ways to get others to review your book.

CHAPTER 6

Building Your Author Brand

Defining Your Author Identity

Defining your identity as an author is a crucial component of your indie publishing journey, as it shapes how you present yourself to readers and the market. Research has shown that it takes three published books to establish an author's identity fully.

1. An author's identity encompasses your writing style, themes, and the values you want to communicate through your work.
2. To effectively establish this identity, begin by reflecting on your personal experiences, interests, and the specific messages you wish to convey.
3. Consider how your background influences your writing and what unique perspectives you bring to your chosen niche.
4. Understanding this foundational aspect will help you articulate who you are as an author and what sets you apart in a crowded marketplace.

Once you have a clear sense of your identity, it is essential to translate that into a consistent, authentic author brand. This brand should be evident across all your platforms, including your website, social media, promotional materials, and business cards. Companies like Artlogo, WiseStamp, and Photologo will give you a unique signature for your promotional materials. It is cost-effective and gives you an additional edge over the competition.

Choose a visual aesthetic that resonates with your writing style and target audience. Your brand is more than a logo on a business card. It is how you want your readers to perceive you. Authenticity is key; for example, if you are writing paranormal fiction, you would like your identity to reflect that. On the other hand, if you want others to perceive you as an inspirational author who genuinely cares about people, your brand should reflect that.

What do I mean by an authentic author brand? Suppose you are an inspirational writer who maintains that you value diversity. Yet, the only diversity you share is quotes by black people during Black History Month or a quote by a Native American once a year on Indigenous People's Day. In that case, you are not authentic about your commitment to diversity. It is a travelogue approach to diversity, and readers will quickly figure that out.

Your author bio should reflect your personality and the themes in your work, providing potential readers with a snapshot of what they can expect. Consistency in your messaging and visual identity strengthens your brand and fosters trust and recognition among your readers. Your bio must also reflect what you are writing. For example, when I write nonfiction, my bio reflects my education and credentials, and when I write a children's book, my bio is more whimsical and fun. I haven't changed; both bios are mine and just different sides of me.

Look at the two examples below and see if you can determine the difference in tone and what I hope to convey in each one.

Non-fiction biography:

Clarissa A. Willis is a professor emerita of Special Education at the University of Southern Indiana. Formerly, she was the Senior Vice President of Education for Kaplan Early Learning Company. Dr. Willis is the senior author of *Learn Every Day: The Program for Infants, Toddlers, and Twos* and *Learn Every Day: The Preschool Curriculum,* two new comprehensive curriculum projects. She is the author of thirteen teacher resource books, including *Teaching Young Children with Autism Spectrum Disorder* (Gryphon House), *Inclusive Literacy Lessons* (Gryphon House), *Teaching Infants Toddlers and Twos with Special Needs (Gryphon House), The Early Childhood Classroom* (Frog Street Press); *My Child has Autism* (Gryphon House), and *Creating Inclusive Learning Environments for Young Children: What to do on Monday morning!* (Corwin Press). She also wrote for McGraw-Hill Early Childhood Division and the Scholastic RED training Project. Her research on autism and early childhood development has been published in journals such as *Teaching Young Children* and *Young Children.*

She speaks nationally and internationally on brain research, early childhood special education, and best practices in early childhood education. She was invited to the President's Conference on Brain Research and Early Childhood Education held at the White House in Washington, D.C. She earned a Ph.D. in Early Childhood Special Education from the University of Southern Mississippi in Hattiesburg, Mississippi. Dr. Willis is a former kindergarten teacher and a licensed Speech-Language Pathologist. She believes in educating all children through exploration and discovery.

Fiction-Biography

Clarissa (Chrissy) Willis is the product of a minister and a drama teacher. She has always had an active imagination and enjoys speaking and writing. She's lived in nine states. She was a major corporation's senior vice president of publishing and has been an educator for over 40 years. As a child growing up in Little Rock, Arkansas, she wrote stories and got into trouble for a variety of mishaps, from the attempted murder of her brother, a crime she swore wasn't her fault, to robbing the collection plate at church.

She earned a PhD in Early Childhood Special Education from the University of Southern Mississippi. In her professional life, Dr. Willis has provided workshops and keynote addresses in all 50 states and three foreign countries. She is a professor emerita from the University of Southern Indiana. Clarissa has written curricula for Frog Street Press, Kaplan Early Learning Company, and Scholastic. She has authored nineteen teacher resource books, including the award-winning *Teaching Young Children with Autism Spectrum Disorder.* In addition, she has written five children's books and is working on a memoir. In her spare time, she serves on the board for Ozark Creative Writers, Between the Pages Writers Conference, and the Missouri Writers' Guild. She lives with her dogs, George and Gracie, in the Ozark Mountains of Northwest Arkansas.

In defining your author identity, it is also essential to consider your target audience. For example, if you're writing paranormal, you might emphasize how you became interested in the genre. If you're writing westerns, your bio might reflect your first trip to the West or how you grew up watching Westerns on TV. Understanding who you are writing for will help you tailor your content and marketing strategies to meet their needs and expectations.

Developing a personal writing philosophy is another key element in establishing your author identity. This philosophy should encapsulate your beliefs about writing, storytelling, and the role of an author in society. Whether you prioritize authenticity, creativity, or message-driven narratives, articulating your philosophy will guide your writing process and decision-making. It will also serve as a foundation for your promotional efforts, allowing you to communicate your values clearly to potential readers.

Mention what made you develop a passion for what you are writing about. Tell the reader something interesting about you so they feel you are someone they would like to sit down and visit with.

Finally, remember that your author identity is not static; it can evolve as you grow as a writer. Embrace the changes that come with new experiences, insights, and shifts in your writing focus. Regularly revisiting and refining your identity will ensure it remains relevant to you and your audience. Maintaining an authentic and adaptable author identity will better position you to navigate the indie publishing landscape and achieve long-term success in your writing career.

Creating a Professional Website

Creating a professional website is essential for authors looking to establish a strong online presence and connect with their audience. A well-designed website serves as a central hub for your brand, providing potential readers with information about your books, background, and upcoming events. The key components of an effective author website include the following:

1. An engaging homepage
2. An informative about page
3. A dedicated section for your books
4. A blog or news section to keep your audience updated

5. Links to your newsletter
6. A contact me page

By carefully curating these elements, you can create a site that reflects your unique voice and aligns with your writing niche.

The homepage is a visitor's first impression of your website, so it's crucial to make it visually appealing and informative. Use high-quality images, including a professional author photo and book covers, to draw attention. Incorporate a straightforward navigation menu that lets visitors quickly find the information they seek. Consider including a brief welcome message or an enticing tagline encapsulating your writing style and genre. This approach sets the tone for the rest of the site and encourages visitors to explore further.

An about page allows you to share your story and connect with readers personally. This section should include your biography, highlighting your writing journey, accomplishments, and any relevant experiences contributing to your credibility as an author. Including personal anecdotes can help humanize your brand and foster a deeper connection with your audience. Remember to keep the tone consistent with your overall professional, casual, or humorous brand. Engaging storytelling in this section can significantly affect how potential readers perceive you and your work.

A dedicated section for your books is vital for showcasing your published works and driving sales. Present each book with an attractive cover image, a captivating synopsis, and links to purchase options. If applicable, include reviews or testimonials to prove your writing's quality. Additionally, consider offering sample chapters or excerpts to give readers a taste of your writing style. This promotes your books and creates an interactive experience that encourages visitors to engage with your content.

Finally, incorporating a blog or news section can enhance your website's appeal by offering fresh content and informing readers about your current projects or adventures. Regularly updating this section with articles on writing tips, industry insights, or personal reflections can establish you as a knowledgeable figure in your niche. Engaging with your audience through comments or social media links can also foster a community around your work. A well-maintained blog improves your website's SEO and keeps readers returning for more, ultimately driving sales and strengthening your author brand.

Engaging with Readers and Fans

Engaging with readers and fans is critical to achieving success in indie publishing. Authors must recognize that the relationship between them and their audience is not merely transactional; it is a dynamic interaction that can significantly influence sales and the longevity of their writing careers. Creating a loyal fan base requires authors to go beyond the initial sale of their books. It involves fostering a community where readers feel valued, heard, and connected to the author's journey. This engagement can take many forms, including social media interactions, newsletters, and author events, each providing unique opportunities to build rapport and trust. I avoid engaging in social media about subjects like politics or religion, as these are deeply personal, and you want a broad fan base.

Social media platforms have revolutionized the way authors can connect with their audiences. It's not just about promoting your work, it's about sharing your journey and making a personal connection. Regularly posting engaging content, responding to comments, and actively participating in discussions can create a sense of familiarity and personal connection. This approach keeps readers informed and encourages them to invest emotionally in your brand, leading to higher engagement and increased book sales.

Newsletters are powerful tools for building intimate relationships with readers. By offering a subscription option on your website, you can create a direct line of communication with your fans. A well-crafted newsletter, filled with exclusive content such as sneak peeks of upcoming releases, personal anecdotes, writing tips, and special promotions, can make your readers feel like insiders in your creative process. This exclusivity and personal touch can foster a deeper connection with your readers.

Participating in both online and in-person author events can significantly boost reader engagement. Book signings, readings, and literary festivals allow authors to meet their fans face-to-face, fostering a stronger connection. Online events, such as webinars or virtual book clubs, enable authors to reach a wider audience while maintaining an interactive environment. These events serve as platforms for authors to discuss their work, answer questions, and engage in meaningful conversations with readers. Such interactions humanize the author and create memorable experiences, motivating readers to advocate for their work.

Ultimately, engaging with readers and fans creates a lasting relationship built on trust and authenticity. Authors who prioritize this engagement will probably see a return on their investment through loyal readers eager to support their future projects. By leveraging social media, newsletters, and events, authors can cultivate a vibrant community around their work, ensuring their journey from manuscript to marketplace is successful and fulfilling. Emphasizing this aspect of the indie publishing process will empower authors to embrace their role as writers and community builders in their respective niches.

The Elephant's Trunk

1. Defining your author identity is essential in creating your brand.
2. A strategically planned professional website gives readers an inside look at who you are as an author.
3. Look for new ways to engage with your readers and build a broader reader base.

CHAPTER 7

Distribution Channels

Choosing the Right Platforms for Distribution

Choosing the proper distribution platforms is a critical step in indie publishing that can significantly affect an author's success. With numerous options available, assessing each platform's strengths and weaknesses is essential. When selecting a distribution channel, remember your specific goals and target audience. Factors such as reach, ease of use, and royalty structures should be considered to ensure that your book is accessible to your intended readers while also maximizing your potential earnings.

One of the most popular platforms for indie publishing is Amazon Kindle Direct Publishing (KDP). It offers a vast audience, as Amazon is one of the largest online retailers in the world. KDP allows authors to publish eBooks, and paperbacks. You can also publish a hardback book on KDP if it has 75 pages. This platform also provides marketing and sales tracking tools. However, it is essential to understand the implications of exclusivity if you enroll in KDP Select, which requires your eBook to be exclusive to Amazon for a set period. This could limit your book's exposure on other platforms, so authors should weigh the benefits against the potential drawbacks. For instance, while KDP does offer you a free ISBN, please do not use it. If you use the free ISBN, you are locked into Amazon, limiting your ability to put your books on other platforms. It's essential to consider these factors when deciding on your distribution strategy.

The place to purchase your ISBNs is Bowker. Please note that you do not need to buy a barcode or copyright your book at Bowker. The barcode is free and is added by your publisher (KDP, IngramSpark). If you use a publishing service, they often will provide ISBNs at a significantly reduced price since they purchase them in bulk from Bowker. If you buy them individually from Bowker they are $125 each.

Authors can leverage other significant platforms to distribute their work beyond Amazon. IngramSpark is a popular choice for authors looking to reach bookstores and libraries, as it offers extensive distribution channels. This platform allows authors to publish print and eBooks and has a reputation for high-quality print services. Platforms like Smashwords and Draft2Digital also facilitate broad distribution to retailers like Apple Books, Barnes & Noble, and Kobo. Each platform has unique features, so it is crucial to evaluate how they align with your distribution strategy.

I use a combination of the two. I use KDP for my paperback books and IngramSpark for my hardback books. Each book (hardcover, paperback, eBook) requires a unique ISBN. Several author sites tell indie authors that eBooks do not need an ISBN, and this is true unless you plan to register your book with the Library of Congress.

Independent authors can get a pre-published Library of Congress number for their copyright page. It is free, and having one shows that you are a professional, and you know that libraries and schools will not buy your book unless you have one. To get a pre-published Library of Congress number, you can visit the Library of Congress website and follow the instructions for the Preassigned Control Number program.

https://maint.loc.gov/publish/prepubbooklink/.

This number is a unique identifier for your book and can enhance your book's credibility.

Another consideration is the increasing importance of direct sales through personal websites or social media. Building a strong author brand enables you to cultivate a loyal readership and sell directly to consumers, which can lead to higher profit margins. Utilizing platforms like Shopify or Gumroad can make setting up a storefront on your website more manageable, giving you complete control over pricing and customer engagement. Direct sales also allow you to keep a larger share of your profits and build a more personal connection with your readers. By selling directly, you can offer special promotions, personalized messages, and unique content to your readers, enhancing their experience and loyalty to your brand.

Some authors do sell on their websites. Once your indie published book is on a platform, you can order author copies at a reduced price (plus shipping) to sell on your website or use for author events. Many authors make the lion's share of their profits from local craft fairs and book signings. This is why the benefits of indie publishing far outweigh the benefits of using a hybrid publisher. A hybrid publisher will sell you author copies of your books but with a built-in profit for themselves. As an indie published author, you can purchase your author copies at a much lower cost from platforms like KDP and IngramSpark.

Ultimately, choosing distribution platforms should align with your marketing strategy and business goals. Authors should conduct thorough research to understand where their target audience spends time and how they prefer to purchase books. By diversifying distribution across multiple platforms, indie published authors can reach a wider audience while mitigating risks associated with reliance on a single source. This strategic approach enhances visibility and fosters long-term success in the competitive landscape of indie publishing.

Understanding Print vs. Digital Options

Understanding the differences between print and digital options is essential for authors navigating the indie publishing landscape. Each format presents unique advantages and challenges that can significantly affect a book's visibility, accessibility, and sales. Print options include traditional physical formats such as paperbacks and hardcovers, while digital options encompass eBooks and audiobooks. Authors should consider their target audience, marketing strategies, and personal preferences when deciding which formats to pursue.

Print books have a tactile appeal that many readers cherish. Holding a physical book, flipping through its pages, and displaying it on a shelf can create a sense of ownership and connection that digital formats often lack. Additionally, print books can be sold at local bookstores, libraries, and events, allowing authors to engage directly with readers. Print options can be particularly advantageous for authors targeting niche markets that value physical copies, such as collectors or specific genre enthusiasts.

On the other hand, digital formats offer unparalleled convenience and reach. eBooks can be instantly downloaded across various devices, making them accessible to a global audience without the limitations of shipping and inventory. This immediacy can increase sales volumes, especially when authors employ effective digital marketing strategies. Furthermore, digital platforms often provide authors with tools to analyze sales data and reader engagement, allowing for informed adjustments to marketing efforts and future projects.

Another key consideration is the cost structure associated with each format. Print books typically involve upfront costs for printing, distribution, and potentially storage, depending on the print run. These costs can be a barrier for new authors, but they also provide the possibility of higher profit margins per sale if managed effectively. In contrast, digital indie publishing often requires a lower initial investment and minimal ongoing costs, enabling authors to experiment with pricing and promotional strategies without significant financial risk.

Ultimately, many authors successfully adopt a hybrid approach that includes print and digital formats. This strategy allows them to capitalize on the strengths of each medium, reaching diverse audiences while maximizing their market potential. By carefully assessing their goals, target demographic, and the nature of their content, authors can make informed decisions that enhance their indie publishing success and build a robust author brand in an increasingly competitive marketplace.

Global Distribution Strategies

Global distribution strategies are crucial for authors aiming to maximize their reach and impact in indie publishing. Understanding international market trends helps authors connect with diverse readers and grow their brand presence. By utilizing different platforms and distribution channels, authors can manage the complexities of global markets and ensure their work reaches a wider audience.

One practical approach to global distribution is utilizing aggregator services that facilitate access to multiple international bookstores and e-commerce platforms. These services can streamline getting books into various markets, allowing authors to focus on their writing and marketing efforts. Aggregators often provide insights into which regions are most receptive to specific genres, enabling authors to tailor their promotional strategies accordingly. This not only saves time but also enhances the likelihood of achieving sales in different countries.

Besides using aggregators, authors should consider the unique preferences and cultural nuances of international audiences. Researching local reading habits, popular genres, and pricing structures can inform authors how to position their work effectively. For example, some cultures may prefer print books over eBooks, while others may have specific formats or cover designs that resonate better. By adapting their approach based on these factors, authors can create a more appealing product for international readers.

Networking with international communities and participating in global book fairs can further enhance distribution efforts. These events allow authors to showcase their work and build relationships with foreign publishers, agents, and readers. Connecting with other authors can also yield insights into successful strategies that have worked in specific markets. Engaging in social media platforms and online communities that cater to international audiences can create additional pathways for visibility and sales.

Lastly, authors must remain vigilant about global distribution's legal and logistical aspects. This includes understanding copyright laws, tax implications, and shipping considerations for physical books. Authors should also know different platforms and countries' varying terms and conditions. By proactively addressing these challenges, authors can establish a sustainable and successful global distribution strategy that supports their long-term indie publishing goals.

International Rights vs International Distribution

There is a difference between international rights and international distribution. If you use IngramSpark or Lulu to publish your book, they offer expanded distribution internationally. That means they will distribute your book in English to other countries. While it is crucial to allow returns when distributing books in the United States, I strongly recommend that you do not offer returns on international sales as the shipping can be costly. International rights are entirely different from international distribution.

Every year, there are international rights trade shows, the largest of which is the Frankfurt Book Fair in Germany. At those fairs, publishers from other countries buy rights to publish your book in their language. The process is very similar to when a producer in Hollywood buys the option to make a movie from a novel. These publishers give you (or your representative) money to publish your book in their language. Whether the book is ever published or not, you get to keep the money. Your only obligation is to agree not to sell that book to another publisher who publishes books in that language.

It is essential, however, to have an international rights representative manage this process to ensure the contract is fair and that your book is not provided to the buyer until money has been received and converted to US currency. These representatives will usually charge anywhere from (25-50%) to handle your book. While this may seem high, remember that your representative must pay to travel to these shows and secure space to display your book. Shelves or stands at international shows can run anywhere from several thousand dollars to tens of thousands of dollars. In addition, your representative must also pay to ship the books to the show. Beware of an international rights representative that claims they can sell international rights for your books without attending the international book fairs. While the internet has made the international rights business more manageable, most rights buying still occurs when your book is physically displayed at a show.

If you are an indie author genuinely interested in international rights, I strongly encourage you to join the International Book Publishers Association (IBPA). They offer opportunities for international rights venues and keep an ongoing list of reputable rights representatives.

For example, my book *Teaching Young Children with Autism Spectrum Disorder* was displayed at the Frankfurt and Bologna Book Fairs. As a result, publishers from 12 different countries bought the option to publish it. Ten of those countries followed through, and now that book is available in Russian, French, British English, Korean, Italian, Spanish, German, Turkish, Mandarin, and Hebrew.

Granted, what other countries pay for book options is not huge (usually between $1000 and $5000), but it is another revenue stream for indie authors.

International rights are entirely different from global distribution in English and can be an added source of revenue for the indie author.

The Elephant's Trunk

1. Strategically researching distribution channels is vital to discovering which best fits your book.
2. Authors can decide which option best suits them by understanding print vs. digital. Remember that it is possible to use a combination of both.
3. Global distribution consists of the worldwide distribution of your book in English.

CHAPTER 8

Navigating the Indie Publishing Process

Step-by-Step Guide to Indie Publishing

Indie publishing offers a viable route for authors looking to bring their work directly to readers without the traditional constraints of the publishing industry. The first step in the indie publishing journey is to finalize your manuscript. This entails completing your writing and engaging in thorough editing and proofreading. If you are in a critique group or writing organization, meet with those writing in your niche or genre. Hone your craft before you even consider publishing. Network with others, ask for advice from trusted friends and other authors, and ultimately decide what path you want to take for your book.

1. Once your manuscript is as good as it can be, it's time to consider editing. Hiring a professional editor ensures your manuscript is polished and error-free. A well-edited book enhances readability and elevates your credibility, which is crucial for building your author brand. As

mentioned, your manuscript should be content-edited and line-edited (proofread) before.

2. Find a professional book designer to lay out your book. Depending on their background, this person or service may help you with the cover art. But remember, the two things that sell the book are the front cover and the back cover.

3. Focus on the design elements of your book. The cover and interior layout are vital in capturing potential readers' attention. Invest in a professional cover designer who understands your genre and can create an eye-catching design that reflects your book's content.

4. Please pay attention to formatting your manuscript for both print and digital versions, ensuring that it meets the specifications of your chosen platform. A visually appealing book attracts readers and enhances the overall reading experience.

Once your manuscript is ready, it's time to explore the various available indie publishing platforms. Familiarize yourself with options like Amazon Kindle Direct Publishing, IngramSpark, and Lulu, each offering unique features and distribution channels. Research their royalty structures, formatting requirements, and distribution networks to determine which platform best suits your goals. Understanding the nuances of each option will empower you to make an informed choice that aligns with your target audience and niche market.

As previously mentioned, marketing your indie published book is as critical as the writing and publishing process. Develop a marketing strategy to build an online presence through social media, author websites, and email newsletters. Engage with your audience by sharing insights into your writing process and updates about your book.

Consider utilizing content marketing techniques, such as blogging or guest posting in niche markets like romance, travel or education, to establish your authority and broaden your reach. Networking with other authors and participating in relevant online communities can provide invaluable support and promotional opportunities.

Finally, after launching your book, continuously seek feedback and adapt your marketing strategies. This ongoing feedback loop, which includes monitoring sales data and reader reviews, empowers you to understand what resonates with your audience. It helps you improve your book and guides future writing projects. Cultivating a long-term relationship with your readers is essential for sustained success in indie publishing. By remaining engaged and responsive, you can build a loyal fan base to support your work and contribute to your growth as an author.

Common Pitfalls to Avoid

One of the most significant pitfalls authors face during indie publishing is neglecting the importance of a professional cover design. It's crucial to be aware that many writers underestimate the impact of visual presentation, assuming that a simple design or a DIY approach will suffice. However, the cover is often the first point of contact for potential readers, and a poorly designed cover can deter them from even considering the book. Investing in a professional designer who understands the genre and target audience can substantially enhance the book's marketability, making it more appealing and credible.

Another common mistake is failing to conduct thorough market research before launching a publication. Authors often pour their energy and creativity into writing without analyzing their target audience and competitors. Understanding the niche market is crucial for positioning the book effectively. Authors should identify similar titles, study their strengths and weaknesses, and determine what unique angle their book offers. This research will inform marketing strategies and help authors avoid oversaturation in a competitive market.

Many authors also overlook the importance of a solid marketing plan. Indie publishing does not guarantee visibility; therefore, creating a comprehensive strategy that includes pre and post-launch activities is essential. This plan should encompass social media promotion, email marketing, and collaborations with influencers within the niche. A well-structured marketing plan ensures consistent promotion, significantly enhances book visibility, and increases sales by reaching a wider audience and maintaining reader engagement.

Authors must also avoid inadequate editing. While the excitement of completing a manuscript can tempt writers to rush to publication, thorough editing is essential for ensuring quality and professionalism. Indie publishing authors should ideally invest in developmental and copy editing to refine their work. Hiring professional editors can help identify plot inconsistencies, grammatical errors, and awkward phrasing, ultimately leading to a polished final product that resonates with readers.

Recognize that the back blurb sells your book. If you tell the whole story, readers will probably ask themselves, Why should I buy this book? I already know what happens? Your back cover is your first and, in some ways, most important marketing strategy. There are tools to help you write your back cover blurb, such as the Kindlepreneur Book Description Generator and other AI tools built into programs like Grammarly and Canva.

Build an author brand. Finally, many authors fail to build an author brand before launching their book. A strong author brand establishes credibility and fosters a connection with the audience. This involves creating a cohesive online presence through a personal website and social media channels that reflect the author's voice and values. Engaging with readers, sharing insights into the writing process, and providing valuable content can help authors cultivate a loyal following. By prioritizing brand building, authors set the stage for long-term success in indie publishing and can more effectively navigate the challenges of the marketplace.

Resources for Indie Authors

Indie authors can access many resources that can significantly enhance their publishing journey. Understanding the various tools and services available can help authors streamline their processes, improve their book quality, and increase their visibility in the marketplace. Authors must equip themselves with the right resources to navigate the indie publishing landscape effectively, from editing and design services to marketing strategies and distribution channels.

One of the fundamental aspects of indie publishing is ensuring that the manuscript is polished and professional. Authors can benefit from hiring freelance editors specializing in different editing stages, such as developmental, copyediting, and proofreading. Platforms like Reedsy and Fiverr offer access to experienced editors who can provide valuable feedback and help refine the manuscript. Additionally, utilizing beta readers or critique partners can offer insights from a reader's perspective, ensuring the book resonates with its target audience.

As mentioned, many reputable companies provide author support and offer various services, from editing to book design. For a complete list of author services, consult the Alliance of Independent Authors (ALLi). ALLi also hosts a watchdog service identifying predatory services that authors should avoid.

Design is another crucial element that indie publishing authors need to focus on. A professionally designed cover can make a significant difference in attracting readers.

Services like 99designs and BookCoverZone provide opportunities to work with talented designers who understand market trends and can create eye-catching covers. Furthermore, quality interior formatting is essential for a polished final product. Tools like Scrivener and Vellum can assist authors in formatting their books for various platforms, ensuring the reading experience is seamless across devices.

Marketing and promotion are vital components of a successful indie publishing strategy. Authors should familiarize themselves with various marketing tools and platforms to amplify their reach. Social media platforms like Instagram and Blue Sky offer opportunities for authors to connect with readers and build a community around their brand. Additionally, services like Mailchimp, Constant Contact, and iConnect can help authors create mailing lists to keep their audience updated on new releases and promotions. Understanding Search Engine Optimization (SEO) and leveraging keywords for online visibility can also significantly drive traffic to an author's website or book sales page.

Finally, authors should explore distribution options to maximize their book's availability. Indie publishing platforms like Amazon Kindle Direct Publishing, IngramSpark, and Draft2Digital offer diverse distribution channels that can help authors reach a broader audience. Each platform has different advantages, so authors should evaluate their needs and choose the one that aligns with their goals. Engaging with author communities, such as forums and social media groups, can provide insights and support throughout this process, as experienced authors often share tips and tricks for navigating the indie publishing world.

The Elephant's Trunk

1. Indie publishing requires the author to stay informed and to understand various distribution models.
2. Authors should learn about new software to enhance their indie journey.
3. Reputable publishing services can guide you through the Indie Publishing process.

CHAPTER 9

Post-Publication Strategies

Monitoring Sales and Feedback

Monitoring sales and feedback is a crucial aspect of the indie publishing journey that authors must prioritize to ensure success in a competitive market. After investing time and effort in crafting a manuscript, understanding how it performs can provide valuable insights for future projects. Sales figures reveal a title's financial viability and marketing strategies' effectiveness. By analyzing sales data across different platforms, authors can identify trends, peak sales periods, and even the impact of promotional efforts. This information is essential for making informed decisions about pricing, distribution, and targeted marketing campaigns.

Authors can effectively track sales and gather feedback by using analytics tools. Many indie publishing platforms offer dashboards that allow authors to monitor sales in real time, providing insight into which titles are performing well, and which ones may need additional marketing efforts. If you use KDP or IngramSpark to publish your book, there are built-in tools to help you analyze more than just how many books you have sold.

Authors can also use tools like Google Analytics to track website or blog traffic, enabling them to see how their promotional strategies resonate with potential readers. Other analytic tools include Hotjar, Matomo (previously Piwik), Crazy Egg and Adobe Analytics. By regularly reviewing these analytics, authors can adapt their marketing strategies, ensuring they align with reader preferences and market demands. Feedback from readers is equally important as it shapes an author's understanding of their audience and their work's reception. Platforms like Amazon, Goodreads, and various social media outlets provide spaces for readers to share their thoughts.

Authors should actively engage with this feedback, noting positive reviews and constructive criticism. Positive feedback can serve as a motivational tool, while constructive criticism can highlight areas for improvement. This dual approach helps refine writing skills and fosters a sense of community and connection with readers, which can be invaluable for building a loyal audience. Be prepared for a bad review; sometimes, a reader gets angry and leaves you a one-star review for no apparent reason. Accept that it happens and move on. Unless you get multiple one-star reviews, it might be time to look at why readers are not connecting with your material.

Engaging with readers through surveys and feedback can also improve an author's understanding of their audience. By seeking direct input from readers, authors can gather specific insights about what resonated in their books and what they want to see in future works. This proactive approach shows that the author values their readers' opinions and helps create a more personalized writing experience. As authors refine their craft based on reader feedback, they can strengthen their author brand and increase the chances of repeat readers.

Finally, consistent monitoring of sales and feedback should be seen as an ongoing process rather than a one-time task. The publishing landscape is ever evolving, and what works today may not be as effective tomorrow. Authors should remain adaptable, using the insights garnered from their sales data and reader feedback to pivot their strategies as necessary. By embracing a continuous improvement mindset, authors can enhance indie publishing success and foster a sustainable writing career.

Planning for Future Projects

Planning for future projects is crucial to an author's journey, especially in indie publishing. Authors must recognize that each book is a standalone piece and part of a larger career narrative. By strategically planning future projects, writers can create a cohesive brand that resonates with their target audience. This involves understanding market trends, reader preferences, and personal writing goals. A well-structured plan can help identify which niches to explore, ensuring that each new project builds on the previous successes while expanding the author's reach.

One practical approach to planning future projects is conducting thorough market research. This involves analyzing current trends in the publishing industry, including popular genres, emerging themes, and reader demographics. Authors can tailor their writing to meet these needs by staying informed about market demands. Tools such as reader surveys, social media polls, and keyword research can provide valuable insights into what readers seek. This data not only aids in selecting the next project but also helps position it effectively within the competitive landscape of indie publishing.

Establishing a timeline for future projects can enhance productivity and focus, besides market research. Authors should consider their writing speed, available resources, and personal commitments when setting deadlines. Creating a project timeline that outlines key milestones, such as drafting, editing, and marketing phases, can help manage expectations and maintain momentum. By breaking down larger projects into manageable tasks, authors can ensure they remain on track while allowing flexibility for unforeseen challenges or opportunities.

Building an author brand is another critical component of planning for future projects. A cohesive brand helps establish a recognizable identity that readers can connect with. This involves consistent messaging across various platforms, including social media, websites, and book covers. Authors should think about how each new project contributes to their overall brand and consider ways to incorporate elements that resonate with their audience. Whether it's a specific theme, character type, or writing style, ensuring that future projects align with the established brand can enhance reader loyalty and engagement.

Finally, authors should recognize the importance of networking and collaboration in planning. Connecting with other writers, industry professionals, and readers can offer new perspectives and ideas for upcoming projects. Attending writing workshops, conferences, or local author events can build relationships that lead to collaborative opportunities or valuable mentorship. By fostering a supportive community, authors can gain insights that improve their planning and help them better navigate the challenges of indie publishing. In this changing landscape, the ability to adapt and innovate through collaboration can greatly influence an author's success.

Leveraging Success for New Opportunities

Leveraging success for new opportunities is essential for authors who have navigated the indie publishing landscape and achieved a measure of success. This success does not merely signify the completion of a manuscript or the publication of a book; it represents a critical juncture where authors can capitalize on their achievements to explore new avenues for growth. By analyzing the elements that contributed to their success, authors can identify transferable skills and insights that can be applied to future projects, whether they are new book ideas, collaborations, or ventures within the writing industry.

One effective strategy for leveraging success is to build a strong author brand. A recognizable brand can be a foundation for future projects, enabling authors to create a loyal readership eager for new releases. This involves consistent branding across all platforms and engaging with readers through social media, newsletters, and other channels. Authors can share their journeys, insights, and challenges, fostering a connection that can lead to more significant support for subsequent works. A well-crafted author brand can be a powerful tool for attracting new opportunities and collaborations.

Moreover, successful authors can transform their experiences into educational content or workshops, sharing their expertise with aspiring writers. This positions them as thought leaders in indie publishing and opens opportunities for additional income sources. By hosting webinars, creating writing guides, or offering one-on-one coaching, authors can leverage their success to help others, building a community that values their knowledge and experiences. This strengthens their brand and establishes them as trusted resources within niche markets.

Networking remains a vital part of achieving success. Authors who have found success in indie publishing should proactively build connections within the literary community, including other writers, editors, and industry experts. Attending book fairs, participating in author panels, and engaging in online forums can create valuable relationships that might lead to collaborations, promotional opportunities, or introductions to literary agents and publishers. Developing a strong network can boost an author's visibility and credibility, opening the door to future achievements.

Finally, reflection and adaptability are key to leveraging success for new opportunities. Authors should regularly evaluate their past projects to understand what resonated with their audience and what strategies were most effective. This reflection can guide their future writing endeavors, helping them to remain relevant in a constantly evolving market. By staying attuned to industry trends and audience preferences, authors can pivot their strategies and explore new genres, formats, or even multimedia projects, ensuring that their journey in indie publishing continues to thrive.

The Elephant's Trunk

1. Authors should monitor reader feedback and analyze sales data to determine what is not working.
2. Branding must always be considered when planning new projects.
3. Networking with other writers and industry professionals can open up new opportunities and collaborations.

CHAPTER 10

The Future of Indie Publishing

Trends Shaping the Industry

The indie publishing industry is evolving rapidly, influenced by technological advancements, changing consumer behaviors, and the increasing accessibility of publishing tools. One notable trend is the rise of digital platforms facilitating indie publishing. Authors now have access to many services that enable them to publish their work with no traditional publishing houses. This has empowered writers to retain creative control and a larger share of their profits. As a result, more authors are exploring innovative ways to present and market their books, leading to a more diverse literary landscape. But this is a cautionary tale because there is a point where a writer becomes an author. While this may seem to be synonymous, it is not. A writer is someone who writes, and an author treats their writing like a business and publishes market-worthy books.

Another significant trend is the increasing importance of data analytics in understanding reader preferences and market trends. Authors are now equipped with tools that provide insights into reader demographics, purchasing habits, and feedback. This data-driven approach enables them to tailor their content and marketing strategies more effectively. Authors can identify niche markets that align with their writing style and target audience by analyzing trends and consumer behavior. This strategic focus enhances the potential for sales and fosters stronger connections with readers seeking specific genres or themes.

The growth of social media and digital marketing has transformed how authors build their brands and connect with their audiences. Platforms like Instagram, X, and Facebook allow authors to engage directly with readers, share their writing journeys, and promote their books. This shift towards personal branding is essential for indie published authors, as it helps them establish a recognizable presence in a crowded marketplace. By leveraging social media, authors can cultivate a loyal following, generate buzz around new releases, and foster a sense of community among their readers. But just like everything else, social media is a tool that must be learned.

Additionally, the rise of audiobooks and podcasting presents new opportunities for authors to reach wider audiences. The demand for audiobooks has surged, driven by the convenience of consuming content while multitasking. Authors who embrace this trend can increase their readership and explore new storytelling formats. Podcasting allows authors to discuss their books, share insights about their writing process, and connect with fans in an intimate setting. Both mediums allow for creative expression and help authors diversify their revenue streams while enhancing their visibility in the industry. To be successful authors must put themselves out there in more innovative ways, such as offering to speak to a local charity group or connecting with teachers and librarians at an educational conference.

Lastly, the focus on sustainability within the publishing industry is gaining traction. As environmental awareness grows, authors and publishers are increasingly adopting eco-friendly practices. This trend includes using sustainable materials for print books, reducing waste in packaging, and exploring digital alternatives. Authors who align their brand with sustainable practices can appeal to environmentally conscious readers, differentiating themselves in a market that values corporate responsibility. By embracing these trends, authors can not only navigate the complexities of indie publishing but also position themselves for long-term success in an ever-changing industry.

The Role of Technology in Publishing

Technology integration into the publishing industry has transformed how authors create, publish, and market their works. In an age of ubiquitous digital tools, authors can access myriad resources that streamline the publishing process. From writing software that aids in drafting manuscripts to platforms that facilitate indie publishing, technology has democratized the publishing landscape. This shift empowers authors to take control of their narratives and reach audiences that traditional publishing routes may not have accommodated.

One of the most significant advancements in publishing technology is the rise of digital publishing platforms. Services like Kindle Direct Publishing, IngramSpark, and Smashwords allow authors to publish their work without a traditional publisher. This accessibility means that authors can bypass gatekeepers, allowing them to publish niche genres that may not have a broad market appeal. The ability to publish eBooks and print-on-demand titles means that authors can launch their works quickly and with minimal upfront costs, making indie publishing a viable option for many.

Marketing technology also plays a crucial role in an author's success. Social media platforms, email marketing tools, and author websites enable writers to build their brands and connect with readers directly. Social media allows authors to engage with potential readers, share their writing journey, and promote their books. Email marketing platforms help authors maintain relationships with their audience, offering them exclusive content or updates on new releases. Using these tools, authors can cultivate a loyal reader base and enhance visibility in a crowded marketplace.

Additionally, data analytics in publishing has provided authors with previously unavailable insights. Authors can make informed decisions about their writing and publishing strategies by analyzing reader preferences, sales trends, and marketing effectiveness. Understanding which genres are trending or what types of marketing campaigns yield the best results allows authors to tailor their efforts, ensuring they invest time and resources where they will be most effective.

This data-driven approach to publishing is essential for authors aiming to achieve long-term success in their careers.

Finally, technology continuously evolves, and authors must stay informed about new tools and platforms that can aid their publishing journey. Embracing innovations such as artificial intelligence for editing, formatting, and marketing can save time and improve the quality of their work. As the publishing landscape shifts, authors who remain adaptable and open to leveraging technology will be better positioned to thrive. By understanding and utilizing the various technological advancements available, authors can navigate the challenges of indie publishing and enhance their chances of success in the competitive marketplace.

Preparing for an Evolving Market

In the fast-paced publishing world, adapting to an evolving market is crucial for authors seeking a successful indie publishing career. Understanding market trends, reader preferences, and emerging technologies can help authors position themselves effectively within their niche. To prepare for these changes, authors should conduct continuous market research, analyze consumer behavior, and stay updated on industry developments. This proactive approach allows authors to anticipate shifts in demand and adjust their writing and marketing strategies accordingly.

Authors should identify their target audience and understand their specific needs and preferences. This involves recognizing the genres and themes that resonate with readers and analyzing demographic factors such as age, location, and reading habits. Authors can gather valuable insights that inform their writing and promotional efforts by leveraging social media analytics, online surveys, and reader feedback. Tailoring content to meet the evolving interests of their audience can lead to increased engagement and loyalty, ultimately enhancing an author's brand.

Besides understanding their audience, authors must be aware of technological advancements that can affect the publishing landscape. The rise of eBooks, audiobooks, and various digital platforms has transformed how readers consume content. Authors should familiarize themselves with these formats and consider diversifying their offerings to include multiple work formats. Embracing new technologies such as print-on-demand services or utilizing social media for marketing can help authors reach a wider audience and adapt to readers' changing preferences.

Networking with other authors and industry professionals can also be a valuable strategy for navigating an evolving market. Joining writing groups, attending workshops, and participating in literary events can provide authors with insights into current trends and best practices. Building relationships with other writers, editors, and publishers can lead to collaborative opportunities, mentorship, and shared knowledge that can enhance an author's understanding of the market. Establishing a support system within the writing community can be instrumental in staying informed and motivated.

Finally, authors should remain flexible and open-minded to change. The publishing industry is inherently unpredictable, and the most successful authors can pivot their strategies when necessary. Regularly reviewing and reassessing their goals, marketing techniques, and writing styles will help authors stay relevant in a dynamic market. By embracing continuous learning and adaptation, authors can survive and thrive in the competitive indie publishing world, ensuring their voices are heard amidst the ever-evolving literary landscape.

The Role of Artificial Intelligence (AI)

Artificial intelligence (AI) is often criticized as a way to get inexpensive cover designs or instantly available online content. Many professionals view using AI to write on your behalf as unethical and plagiarism. But what about AI tools? Are they also considered unethical? That area is uncertain; in this author's opinion, using AI tools like those that reword or rewrite your content is not unethical because it doesn't create anything new, it simply enhances your work. Grammarly, Canva, and Adobe have AI features integrated into their platforms. When used wisely, they can greatly improve an author's work.

For example, here is a book blurb I wrote for this book:

The Elephant in the Room is written to help indie authors navigate the often-complex world of indie publishing. An author can succeed with easy tips and an understanding of what it takes to publish a book independently. Using technology and tools and building an author brand are also important for an aspiring indie author. This book helps authors learn what they need to do to become successful authors.

The same back book blurb using the AI tool in Canva

The Elephant in the Room is crafted to guide indie authors through the intricate labyrinth of independent publishing. With straightforward tips and insights into the art of indie publication, any author can uncover the path to success. Embracing technology, utilizing essential tools, and cultivating a distinctive author brand are vital for the aspiring indie author. This book empowers authors with the knowledge they need to flourish in an ever-changing and highly competitive market.

For fiction books, the free Kindlepreneur Book Description Generator can be very helpful in creating a back-of-the-book blurb that hooks a potential reader. (https://kindlepreneur.com/amazon-book-description-generator)

Artificial intelligence is becoming more sophisticated every day. ChatGPT has morphed into everything from AI robots you can buy to handle everything from email lists to social media posts. Sintra AI now offers bots for twelve areas from data analytics to social media marketing. In addition, they offer a sales manager, SEO specialist, and virtual assistant. Customers can purchase one or all 12 assistants who work 24 hours to meet their needs. I own Soshie, the social media Bot, and with her help, my book sales have increased dramatically over the past few months. She not only posts about my books, but she also posts interesting information that my readers enjoy.

Finally, authors should remain flexible and open-minded to change. The publishing industry is unpredictable, and the most successful authors can pivot their strategies when necessary. Regularly reviewing and reassessing their goals, marketing techniques, and writing styles will help authors stay relevant in a dynamic market. By embracing continuous learning and adaptation, authors can survive and thrive in the competitive indie publishing world, ensuring their voices are heard amidst the ever-evolving literary landscape.

The Elephant's Trunk

1. The future is bright for indie authors if they stay up to date with new trends and market shifts.
2. Artificial Intelligence is a tool that can enhance your writing, but it is not meant to write for you.
3. The literary landscape is changing, and well-informed indie authors can be successful.

ABOUT THE AUTHOR

Clarissa (Chrissy) Hightower-Willis is the product of a minister and a drama teacher. She has always had an active imagination and enjoys speaking and writing. She's lived in nine states. She was a major corporation's senior vice president of publishing and has been an educator for over 40 years.

As a child growing up in Little Rock, Arkansas, she wrote stories and got into trouble for a variety of mishaps, from the attempted murder of her brother, a crime she swears wasn't her fault, to robbing the collection plate at church.

She earned a PhD in Early Childhood Special Education from the University of Southern Mississippi. In her professional life, Dr. Willis has provided workshops and keynote addresses in all 50 states and three foreign countries. She is a professor emerita from the University of Southern

Indiana.

Clarissa has written curricula for Frog Street Press, Kaplan Early Learning Company, and Scholastic. She has also written four children's books and nineteen teacher resource books, including the award-winning Teaching Young Children with Autism Spectrum Disorder.

In her spare time, she serves on the board for Ozark Creative Writers, Between the Pages Writers Conference, and Sleuths' Ink Mystery Writers. She lives with her dogs, George Maurice and Gracie Girl, in the Ozark Mountains of Northwest Arkansas.